DEDICATION

A special thank you to Muntu and Abina who typed, encouraged, typed, made herbal tea, typed and kept Muntu's green drink in full supply; to Jim Tyrell who insisted on a sincere effort; to Queen Afua and Vy Higgenson who insisted that I start this book; to George Fraser and Les Brown who encouraged until I finished the book; and to Jawanza who actually believed I had something worth publishing. Abina, Aisha, French, Ariana, Khalid, Hershel, Daimion, Jamal, Kiera, the future belongs to you. Be ready.

CONTENTS

Dedication iii

Introduction v

Chapter One
     Revolutin' on the Radio 1

Chapter Two
     In The Beginning Was the Word 15

Chapter Three
     The Balm In Gilead 31

Chapter Four
     From Prominence to Power 51

Chapter Five
     Africentricity to the Rescue 73

Chapter Six
     From Black Rage to a Blueprint for Change . . . 85

Chapter Seven
     Bright Eyed Justice 97

Chapter Eight
     An Open Letter to Black Music Radio and the Music Industry 111

Chapter Nine
     Hip vs. Smart 119

Chapter Ten
     Respect Yourself 127

Chapter Eleven
     Therefore 139

Notes 156

VOICES FOR THE FUTURE

Appreciating the past
in order to understand the present
while planning for the future

Bob Law

Chicago, Illinois

Front Cover illustration by Tony Quaid
Photo by David Jenkins
Copyright © 1998 by Bob Law
First Edition, First Printing

All rights reserved. No part of this book may be reproduced, stored in retrieval systems or transmitted in any form, by any means, including mechanical, electronic, photocopying, recording or otherwise, without prior permission of the publisher.

Printed in the United States of America

ISBN: 0-913543-57-8

INTRODUCTION

NIGHTTALK debuted in 1981 as the nation's first broadcast Black radio talk show broadcast on a daily basis. We were on the air Monday through Friday, 12 midnight to 5 a.m., that would later change to 10 p.m. to 2 a.m. From the start there would be exciting exchanges of ideas between myself and the callers as well as between the callers themselves. Callers found themselves on the phone one on one with people who up to now they loved and idolized from afar, now they were on the phone with people like, Stevie Wonder, Anita Baker, Denzel Washington, and Melba Moore. Phillis Hyman sang happy birthday for a mother who called in to request it for her son, who was in the military, she said she was taping the show to send to him since Phillis was his all-time favorite singer. These kinds of opportunities were not available to Black listeners before and certainly not on a regular basis. In addition NIGHTTALK was the first forum where African Americans could discuss issues of particular interest to the Black community without being attacked by a conservative host.

One day you would be reading about the effort to provide decent housing for poor sharecroppers in Tunica

Mississippi and the next night through NIGHTTALK there would be people from Tunica on your phone. There were also the personalities that often appeared in the headlines like Jesse Jackson, Minister Farrakhan, Rev. Al Sharpton, Congresswoman Maxine Waters, that now through NIGHTTALK were up close and personal on the telephone. NIGHTTALK quickly became the Black community's most significant forum for the discussion and development of ideas and strategies. It was on NIGHTTALK that Jesse Jackson as my Tuesday night co-host, built support for his 1984 presidential run, just as it was on NIGHTTALK that I built support for the 1995 Million Man March. That is where the real power and value of NIGHTTALK began to emerge. Not only did the Black community now have voice, but as I began to listen carefully to these voices, I began to hear a consistent theme. The voices were searching for solutions and providing answers for today's problems. What was developing was a blueprint or a data base, if you will, of information that covered every aspect of life, including health, relationships, politics, economic development, marriage, childhood, womanhood, and manhood. Indeed everything. Furthermore, this data base provided information on how to live our lives in this hostile land. As I listened to the voices from around the country, as I continued to work with organizations and individuals from coast to coast what also became apparent was the wealth of information that was being passed along from generation to generation.

It was in the 1930's when Dr. Carter G. Woodson said that the real issue of African American education is the issue of control. It is the same point being made today by education activists like Kwame Kenyatta of Detroit, Atim Sentwali of Mt. Vernon, New York, and Bill Grace of Kansas City, Missouri. We have always known that education is essential to the self-transformation of Black students, therefore the Black community will have to control the process. I can almost hear Dr. Woodson's voice when he said, "The Negro will never be able to show all of his originality as long as his efforts are directed from without by those who socially proscribe him." It was and it remains a question of control.

If we listen carefully to the progressive voices booming from generation to generation, we discover that the blueprint for a new society may already be in our hands, the flight plan for the future, has already been charted. So why then are Black folks still debating the issues as though we are still at square one? Why are we not benefiting more from the wisdom of our ancestors and from the wisdom of our own collective experiences? It is time we hear the voices that have always been preparing us for the future. After all, theirs was a vision of what we must become.

It was poet Listervelt Middelton who said, "Minute by minute, hour by hour, as you lose your history, you lose your power." This book offers a synthesis of the wisdom of our forebearers and our contemporary experiences. Read this book from cover to cover, then share the information with your friends. History provides an important key to our healing. I know that you, like me, are ready to move forward. Enough of debating the same old issues. It's time we made use of our collective wisdom to make a better life for ourselves, our children, and our communities. Use the information contained in the next few pages to sharpen your sight and tune your hearing so that you can hear the life saving messages with a new respect and determination to apply them.

Bob Law
New York City
1998

CHAPTER ONE

Revolutin' on the Radio

"We must take this sound and make this energy meaningful to our people. Otherwise, it will have meant nothing, will have affected nothing. The force of what we have to say can only be realized in action."

Larry Neal

By the late 1930's, 26 million American households owned at least one radio. On average, American families spent five hours a day listening to their radio. Without a doubt, radio was America's, and indeed the world's, primary source of information and ideas. The voice on the radio interpreted and explained the events of the day and established what was generally accepted as American reality. On those rare occasions in which African Americans were included in the programming, they were cast as maids, cooks, butlers, and chauffeurs, simple childlike buffoons, an illusion White Americans felt it necessary to promote. It wasn't until the late 1940's that a newer image of African Americans as a people with some sense began to emerge.

The serious programming of issues affecting the African American community that exists in many cities today began with the ambitious efforts of Jack I. Cooper on WSBC in Chicago. In 1948 he debuted a program called "Listen Chicago." This talk show featured a guest panel that examined current events. Discussions focused on the nation's growing civil rights movement. Later that same year, WDIA in Memphis launched a show called "Brown America Speaks." The show was hosted by Nat D. Williams, a well known local African American newspaper columnist and a respected high school teacher. The radio station promoted the show as a program that addressed issues from a Black perspective. At that time, however, all Black radio stations were White-owned facilities which emphasized entertainment. They offered a menu of music shows, such as the Tan Town Jamboree in Memphis, the Poppa Stoppa Show in New Orleans, and Dr. Jive in New York City. In fact, blues legend B.B. King started his career as a disc jockey on WDIA in Memphis. In those early days, African American talk radio existed as public affairs programming and was broadcast late nights or Sunday afternoons.

Revolutin' On The Radio

For the most part, talk on Black radio was broadcast one day a week and was treated by station owners as a necessary evil forced on them by an FCC regulation requiring local stations to respond to the social needs of the community. I was introduced to Black talk radio in the 1970's, via a Sunday afternoon show called "Tell It Like It Is," which was on WWRL in New York City and hosted by Bernie McCain. Bernie, who currently does mornings on Washington, DC's, full-time Black talk station WOL-AM, introduced the idea of "activist" talk radio. He not only talked about issues, he actually organized around many of the issues he talked about. One of his successful efforts was a widely acclaimed campaign called "help a junkie bust a pusher," an antidrug program that involved some risk for Bernie, since it angered one or two local drug pushers.

I met Bernie McCain when he invited me to be a guest on his show. My own local organization, IMPAC, was challenging the use of the drug Ritalin in New York City's public schools, and Bernie gave us an opportunity to talk about what we were doing. It was Bernie who gave me my start in radio as his replacement at WWRL when he moved to Oakland, California, to direct programming at KDIA-AM. I was a talk show host whose primary duties were as Public Affairs Director for the station. My show was called "Black Dialogue." I was on the air for two hours, one day per week. Since those early efforts, there have been many changes, and African American talk radio has come into its own as a respected and influential forum.

The September 1996 issue of *Emerge* magazine makes the point that African Americans are dialing into radio talk shows more than ever because the shows give their communities a voice and clout. The great value of Black talk radio is its ability to give voice to a community that would otherwise be voiceless. The success of a number of initiatives in the African American community can be linked directly to Black talk radio. The election of Harold Washington as Chicago's first African American mayor was due to that city's Black talk station, WVON-AM. Enthusiasm for and the support of the Million Man March was fueled by Black talk radio. My own NIGHTTALK, broadcast nationally on the American Urban Radio Network, played one of the more pivotal roles in that success story.

The power and influence of Black talk radio have been demonstrated time and again. Jo Ann Watson, on WCHB in Detroit, helped to increase voter registration and voter participation. Gary Byrd of WLIB-AM in New York helped get the African American community out to vote for David Dinkins, who won the Mayoral seat by three percentage points. Washington, DC's Cathy Hughes, owner of fourteen radio stations and talk show host on one of her own stations, WOL-AM in Washington, DC, organized a citywide protest of the *Washington Post*, which published a terribly distorted article about a young African American DC couple. Her broadcast resulted in the massive return of copies of the Sunday *Post*, which were dumped at the front door of the newspaper's Washington headquarters. Joe Madison, an African American talk host on a white talk station in DC, put the *San Jose Mercury News* story of the CIA's likely involvement of cocaine trafficking in South Central Los Angeles on the front burner in the African American community.

And there are many examples of NIGHTTALK'S influence on a national level: We helped raise $100,000 for an organ transplant for a Kansas City teenager, we financed a summer softball league for children on behalf of the Respect Yourself Youth Organization, and we worked to save the Lorraine Motel, the site of Dr. King's assassination. The Lorraine Motel story is a story worth telling since the curator's of the civil rights museum that currently exists on the site of the old motel only casually refers to Black radio's involvement in the saving of the motel from the auction block. Nor do they mention NIGHTTALK and its parent company at the time, the National Black Network, which was owned by entrepreneurs, Sid Small and Eugene Jackson.

However, for the record, in 1982, I was approached by the Martin Luther King Memphis Memorial Foundation, a group supported by local Memphis businessmen and led by Attorney D'Armey Bailey (now a Judge). The group asked if I would use NIGHTTALK to conduct national appeals for their fund-raising campaign. The Foundation wanted to buy the Lorraine Motel, which was about to be sold at a public auction. The group had already been encouraged by the support from appeals made on WDIA-AM in Memphis, but they felt a national appeal would give their efforts the momentum and visibility the project so desperately needed. They wanted to convert the motel into a Martin Luther King Museum, which I agreed would be much more fitting than the stone marker and plastic flowers that had been placed at the door of Dr. King's room. The plan was to prevent the auction by paying off the debt owed by the motel, and then raise the money to build the Martin Luther King Museum.

Revolutin' On The Radio

I agreed to make the appeal and organize various fundraising events in local communities around the country, in conjunction with my on air activity. I wanted to make one adjustment however. I wanted the museum to be dedicated to the entire civil rights movement, with Dr. King as its centerpiece. The group agreed and we launched a national radio campaign on NIGHTTALK, which at the time was being broadcast from midnight to 5 A.M. on the affiliate stations of the National Black Network. The NIGHTTALK audience also responded by calling the Judge who was to rule on the auction, to assure him that they were donating to the memorial fund and that the money was indeed on the way. On the strength of those phone calls and the renewed and expanded enthusiasm for the project, the Judge delayed the auction, giving the Memorial Foundation a few more days to receive contributions from its new supporters across the country. We were successful! The Martin Luther King Memphis Memorial Foundation was able to buy the motel and the time they needed to raise the additional funds to build the excellent Museum of the Civil Rights Movement that currently exists at the site of the old Lorraine Motel. Strangely enough, there is no mention of the NIGHTTALK radio campaign in any of the museum's literature, nor was a promised plaque installed at the museum's entrance to acknowledge the donations of African Americans around the country. These donations did in fact make the Civil Rights Museum possible.

Acknowledged or not, Black talk radio has come of age. There are full-time Black talk stations in many key American cities, not the least of which is WHAT in Philadelphia, owned by veteran broadcaster Cody Anderson. WHAT-AM, like WOL-AM in Washington, DC operates from a proactive perspective and urges listeners to take action around important issues that might otherwise only be discussed. This is the whole point of Black talk radio. In Detroit, State Representative Ed Vaughn had organized a group called United Black Men, but it was the appeal on WCHB-AM radio that increased the membership overnight to 800 men.

There is however an interesting development that seems to occur on Black talk radio. More than likely, it is the result of a subtle but important difference in Black and White talk radio. White talk radio is reactionary and has perfected the art of scapegoating, with African Americans, Latinos, and the poor as the targets of choice. Most white talk show hosts and their callers spend their energy railing against what and whom they do not like. There is no discussion of the contradictions within the White community. No talk of white-on-white crime. No discussion of domestic violence by White men. No examination of drug use among Whites, or why White women become prostitutes, or what accounts for the large number of White women on welfare. Violence by White policemen is never critically examined. White talk radio seems to exist to reinforce the denial that permeates much of White America.

In contrast, Black talk radio tends to examine the problems in the African American community. We tend to talk much more about African American strategies and the inadequacies of Black leaders than we do about Whites. We talk about what we as African Americans need, and what we must do to get what we need personally and as a community. The conversations on Black talk radio tend to be introspective, for example, Why don't we support African American businesses? or Why aren't we building independent schools? or Why do we trust the education of our children to people who hold them in contempt? and so on. The callers to African American talk shows have become quite adept at analyzing and explaining the dilemmas of being Black in America and for the most part, the comments heard on Black call in shows are thoughtful, well informed, and politically and historically on target.

As a result, many African Americans, both the callers and the large number of listeners who do not call in, are receiving a kind of emotional gratification by talking and listening to each other on the radio. There are many who, after having expressed his or her view, often in the sharpest terms possible feel they have struck a blow for the freedom of African American people worldwide.

When you consider how the civil rights movement and the Black consciousness movement became dominant in the lives of African Americans prior to the advent of full-time Black talk radio, it raises some interesting questions about how we may be inadvertently using talk radio. Rather than organizing, the danger is that the struggle for equity for African Americans may be played out to a large extent by talking on the radio.

As wonderful as Black talk radio is, we must never substitute talk for concrete political and economic action. Case in point: Many talk show callers express the need for African Americans to support Black owned businesses as a way of stimulating economic development in the African American community, often citing historical examples of just such efforts by other racial groups. Nonetheless, getting 100 African American listeners to travel by bus to participate in a shopping tour to recycle their dollars back into their own community remains a painstaking chore. Without question, African American talk radio has proven its power to affect change and stimulate action, but it is a power that must not be dissipated by chatter for chatter's sake.

Callers to Black talk shows are often angry with a self righteousness that comes from their awareness of our history and social reality—and thus their anger is understandable. African Americans are entitled to their anger. The more we understand our history, the more we feel that history, and it weighs heavy on us. As we begin to understand the extent to which social engineering has hindered our forward progress, the angrier we become. The more we examine America's social and political realities, the angrier we become. Indeed the more we probe our history and the history of African people, the more our resentment of European domination widens. As Larry Neal once said, "It had to go down that way. There is a concrete historical reason for everything that we feel."

To this day, the hostile treatment of African Americans remains a source of pain and anger. Black churches are still being firebombed, White policemen are still killing unarmed African Americans under dubious circumstances, we have too many low performing schools, and inadequate health facilities. The sharper the sense of pain, the more acute the anger.

Despite our righteous anger, our self worth cannot be founded on anger and hatred of White people. Unless anger provides the catalyst for intelligent action, it means nothing. In the final analysis, the energies of African Americans must be used to build on what we have learned and experienced. It is a misuse of precious time to constantly direct venom at Whites or at the African Americans who have failed us. Instead we must bring to bear, upon the struggle, all of the wisdom of the voices we have heard in our lifetime. Then our experiences and new consciousness will have meaning. Black talk radio has the potential to free the mind by bringing into your living room, bedroom, car, and wherever your radio might be; today's liberators, armed with ideas, information, and insights. This wonderful tool will accomplish nothing if it simply becomes a sounding board that leads to louder sounds. A forum for a kind of hip political chatter that becomes a substitute for concrete action.

Talk forums should help to solve problems. We can use talk radio to share information and create new constructs. Black talk radio is powerful when it is linked to the African American community's political dynamic. It is powerless when it operates as a replica of white talk radio or when it becomes race neutral. The aim of White talk radio is very different from Black talk radio. Our radio is important when without hesitation it speaks directly to the needs and aspirations of African people. It is effective when courageous broadcasters challenge the constructs of white supremacy everywhere. One of the proudest moments on NIGHTTALK was the night in the early 1980's when we penetrated South Africa's apartheid barriers and put Winnie Mandela on the air and on the phone talking one-on-one with African Americans in cities throughout America. Ms. Mandela was on the air about 20 minutes before the South African government interrupted and shut down her phone. Black talk radio provided the opportunity for Winnie Mandela's voice to be heard.

At its best, Black talk radio is a powerful grassroots think tank in which African Americans can intelligently talk through issues and create blueprints for a radical change. We must guard against it becoming a kind of pop art entertainment like an off Broadway show.

We must reevaluate the traditional role of the communicator. Too often the African American talk show host is neutral on critical issues. The National Association of Black Journalists said they could not join the thousands around the world calling for a new trial for Mumia Abu-Jamal, a Philadelphia journalist accused of killing a White policeman. The African American journalists said that they are only allowed to report news as though they have no link to the historical experiences of their own people. They, therefore, are not allowed an opinion. In short they can *cover* the news, but must not engage in any activity that might *make* news.

Black talk radio is where a cultural arts revolution can begin. It is where discussions that promote respect can be taken to the masses. It is where an African American aesthetic can be explored. It is where the assumptions of white supremacy can be challenged.

Langston Hughes talked about the power of the African American artist / communicator when he urged us to communicate about our people instead of fleeing from them in shame or confusion. Hughes' voice is clear when he said, "There is so much richness in Negro humor, so much beauty in Negro dreams, so much dignity in our struggle, and so much universality in our problems." Langston Hughes' comments are just as relevant today. Black talk radio is powerful when it does not run from it's own Blackness.

CHAPTER TWO

In the Beginning Was the Word

Let the words of my mouth and the meditations of my heart be acceptable in thy sight, Oh Lord, my strength and my redeemer.
Psalms 19-14

According to African philosophy, man has, by the force of his word, dominion over all things. He can change them, make them work for him, and command them. Through NOMMO, the word, man establishes his mastery over all things. All change, all production, and development are affected through the word. "I sow through the word" wrote the West African poet, Bernard Dadie. Jesus said that "man does not live by bread alone, but by every word that proceeds from the mouth of God." In African philosophy, the word itself is a force, and since the word has this power, every word is binding. There are no harmless or meaningless words. Therefore, choose words and phrases carefully, understanding that our very utterances create and continually adjust the emotional climate around us.

The use of negative terms and self-defeating language is all too prevalent in the African American community. Dr. Frantz Fanon's voice for the future says, "One of the psychological consequences suffered by the victim of racism is self hatred and loathing." The demeaning words we use not only reflect that self-hatred, but serve to reinforce it. In a sense, speaking is like planting seeds. If you plant negative words all around you, only doubt, fear, anger, and negative conditions will grow in your life. This negative self-concept works effectively against African American people because it operates subtly.

In fact, a kind of low intensity warfare has been launched against the Black community. It is an attack that is unnoticed until its consequences become apparent. No one makes an announcement saying, "Let's increase alcoholism" or "Let's retard the intellectual development of African American students." Instead, malt liquor is heavily promoted to Black youth, including selling a greater variety of the liquor in Black communities, endorsed and promoted by popular Rap artists, using commercials that suggest that malt liquor will provide power for these youth who feel powerless in the real world. City budgets are created that allocate the majority of education funds into white suburban communities while fewer dollars, older text books, substandard equipment, and teachers with less certification are placed in the Black community.

This low intensity warfare also promotes white supremacy by projecting strength and courage as characteristic of whites, while scheming and failure are promoted as characteristics of Black. Note the current romanticized notions of gangsters and pimps, or players and mack daddies, as they are called, being lifted as acceptable images for Black youth. This assault has been effective because it operates on the level of ideas. Music, billboards, videos, and movies are some of the weapons being used to promote ideas that operate from a negative value system.

This value system is morally bankrupt and destroys life. It is a subtle but relentless attack. Therefore, we must use our own intellectual weapons more effectively. Black literature and Black music must become integral to the African American communities. The artists, poets, filmmakers, rappers, and writers must link their efforts to the liberation struggle of their people. They must go beyond simply reflecting what they see on the street and empower their people to envision instead the greatness of what they can be. Susan Taylor's voice for the future says, "Your thoughts are the seeds that grow the conditions of your life. Whatever you wish to achieve awaits your calling it forth." When we fail to understand the power of the Word, our faith in the possible becomes limited. "Simply put, name it, then claim it!" By speaking certain words and terms, we can inadvertently claim negative and self-defeating ideas.

Baseball historians tell the story of the only African American player on a Yale University baseball team being managed by the legendary Branch Rickey. The young athlete was denied his own room in a white hotel, so Branch Rickey let him sleep in his room. When Rickey entered the room, he found the African American youngster crying and rubbing his skin. "It's my skin, isn't it, Mr. Rickey, it's my skin," he sobbed. A sentiment also expressed in a lyric by Louis Armstrong, "My only sin is in my skin, why am I so Black and blue?"

Have you ever been turned down for a job, promotion, or loan that you were absolutely qualified for? When that occurs, and you are sure that race was the deciding factor, the first response is to say that you were denied because you are Black, thus subtly reaffirming the notion that the sin is in your own skin. But if you are actually

In the Beginning Was the Word

qualified, then you could not possibly be turned down because of who you are. You are denied because of what dwells in the heart and mind of the person who denies you. The fact is, you have never been turned down because of your skin color. You were turned down because someone had a negative opinion about your skin color. You were not denied because you were Black, as much as you were denied because the individual discriminating against you was White. But it is the manner by which we process the information, saying it's my skin or because I'm Black that leads to self-doubt and contempt for oneself. Just as thoughts and words have the power to create doubt and fear, so too can they give life, power, and creativity and create a sense of optimism.

In 1984, during Rev. Jesse Jackson's first run for the Presidency, Lt. Robert Goodman, an African American US airman, was shot down in Syrian air space. He had been arrested by the Syrian government and all but abandoned by the Ford administration, so Jesse decided to go to Syria and negotiate his release. We were in the T.W.A. VIP's lounge at New York's Kennedy airport as Jesse's delegation awaited the flight to Syria. I noticed that Jesse was very calm and confident. Of all the people in the room, he and Robert Goodman's mother seemed most at ease, although they had the most to lose.

If Rev. Jackson failed to negotiate the release of Lt. Goodman, he would have been ridiculed by an already hostile American press and more than likely dismissed as a serious candidate for the Presidency. I asked him how he felt about the risk involved. He answered, "In order to achieve our aspirations, we must be willing to take risks that are equal to those aspirations." Often our accomplishments are limited by our fears and disguised as pragmatism. All too often our aspirations are much greater than our willingness to take the risks necessary to achieve the goal. Jesse understood that the level of success he envisioned could not be achieved without significant risk. In fact, the greater the aspirations, very likely the greater the risk! His willingness to take that risk resulted in the unconditional release of Lt. Goodman and an increase in the international stature of Rev. Jackson.

In my many interviews with powerful and successful people, one of the first things I learned about them was that their attitude was always confident, optimistic, and creative. For instance, the call letters Stevie Wonder chose for his Los Angeles radio station, KJLH, stood for Kindness, Joy, Love, Happiness.

No matter the task or the challenge, once the decision is made to undertake it, we must avoid expressions of doubt and fear. Remember, words have power. So consider with care the words you choose. The universe will respond to the energy you project. If you speak with kindness and optimism, you will discourage the negative energies trying to invade your space. As we say in the Respect Yourself Youth Crusade, "If your mind can conceive it, and your heart can believe it, then your spirit can achieve it!"

Your own genius plus faith in God equals success. God will bless you with the things you desire, but you are invited into a partnership with God in order to achieve your goals. The scripture calls for faith and work. "For as the body without the spirit is dead, so faith without work is dead also" (James 2:26). Faith is your confidence that God will do His part. Your work gives God confidence that you will do your part. In short, the quality of your life is the result of the effort you put into creating the conditions you desire. It all begins with the Word. Your dreams are nourished and developed in your prayers. That is where the words you utter become power. It is in the renewing of your mind where the first and most significant change must occur.

The Apostle Paul offers instructions on how to establish this new mindset. In his epistle to the Phillippians,

Paul teaches, "Whatsoever things are true, whatsoever things are honest, whatsoever things are just, whatsoever things are pure, whatsoever things are lovely, whatsoever things are of good report, if there be any virtue, and if there be any praise, think on those things." (Phillipians 4:8 NKJ)

    The Apostle Paul makes it clear we must avoid mean spirited gossip, lying, harsh language, and cynicism like the type displayed on those provocative TV talk shows and in sensationalist literature, all of which really can have a harmful effect on your psyche and ultimately on your personality being waged against the Black community These are the elements of the new constructs springing from the collective wisdom of our ancestors and forefathers, instructing us to reject self-defeating language, to avoid demeaning and destructive tendencies, reminding us that, as you think, so shall you become. The Twenty-first century is being shaped right now in this final decade of the Twentieth. African people must be a part of that process. In other words, the future belongs to you! But only if you prepare for it.

    It is fitting that one of the most significant events to occur in the final decade of the Twentieth century was initiated by African American men: the Million Man

In the Beginning Was the Word

March. Fraught with a myriad of planning and logistical challenges, the March, held on October 15, 1995, was a huge success. However, it is important to understand the spirit, and therefore, the significance of the March. When Minister Farrakhan called for the March, many visionaries gathered across the country to shape this event into a catalyst for a powerful new movement, one that would be capable of sparking the campaign to renew the African American community. But any examination of the Million Man March must begin by putting the March in a historical and political perspective.

For the organizers of the March, 2nd Chronicles 7:14 really was the basis for calling for such an event. That scripture says, "If my people who are called by my name, would humble themselves and pray, turn from their evil ways and seek my face, then shall they hear from heaven and I will heal their land."

Part of the Black man's reaction to oppression has been the tendency to overcompensate for our feelings of powerlessness, which becomes transferred into a Black male persona, which requires us to act out the illusion of power. It's in our walk, our lack of patience with each other. It's an in-your-face attitude that you see being played out on the streets in the Black face.

23

Whenever I talked with other members of the Million Man March executive committee, it was clear to us that the value in getting African American men to acknowledge our own errors could be quite empowering. In other words, if we did what the scripture called for—"humbling ourselves before God"—we would actually open our hearts to receive the extraordinary power of the Holy Spirit. For African American men, including young gang members, to stand before the world as they did at the Million Man March, took courage as well as strength. How many people, male or female, have been able to just stand before their families and admit to their own errors? It was clear to us that we should call African American men together, to summon the greater strength that we would need to transform our communities.

It was a day of atonement for African American men. We were challenged to correct our mistakes and assume more family and community responsibility. The March was a call for African American men to move with a greater sense of urgency to stabilize both family and community. African American women should not view this call as threatening or divisive. We have a legitimate need to find our strengths and share them with each other. The words spoken that day were powerful, not only

In the Beginning Was the Word

touching the hearts and minds of the men on the mall in Washington, DC, but also touching the millions who watched around the globe via TV and satellite.

Perhaps what might have been confusing for some was that the philosophy guiding the Million Man March was based on the principle and the power of atonement. Conventional leadership asks, How can you gather a million men in the nation's capitol and not ask the government for anything? Conventional political thought fails to recognize the significance of speaking to the spirit. A million praying men sought relief, not from the government, but from God and each other.

African American men understood that the March was a declaration of strength. Although there had been other major marches and demonstrations, non dared to make such a public call just to African American men. Other leaders felt that unless they included the entire African population it would not be successful. They did not feel the same sense of power that Minister Farrakhan and the organizers of the March felt. We knew it would be attacked, but we called for it anyway. We appealed to the strength of African American men. African American men ignored the naysayers, and some even risked their jobs to attend. No one spoke to this generation's sense of manhood quite like that before.

Although there were expressions of fear and resentment from some African American women, most understood the necessity for African American men to regroup among themselves. Many women were pleased to see their men atone and seek God's face in order to gather their own strengths and maximize their potential. African American men must honor their women and children. They should be viewed with high regard and exalted. Atonement is powerful, however, it is only a beginning. It must lead to a new movement, but a new mind is absolutely necessary to build a movement. The Bible reminds us that to be transformed requires the renewing of our minds.

The March dared us to embrace our own best values and traditions and stand before the world and say without hesitation that we are calling on African American men to be good husbands and fathers. The March was not simply to indict Black men. However it was indeed a challenge to brothers to correct mistakes and assume more responsibility for enhancing the quality of life in the Black community. In order to move forward, we would have to hear once again the voice of Dr. Benjamin Mays when he instructed us, "That he who is behind must forever remain behind or run faster than he who is in front." My

In the Beginning Was the Word

friend, Terri Williams, author of *The Personal Touch*, sent me a note that makes the point. It said every morning in Africa, a gazelle wakes up and knows that it must outrun the fastest cheetah, or it will be killed. Every morning a cheetah wakes up and knows it must outrun the slowest gazelle, or it will starve to death. It doesn't make any difference if you are the cheetah or the gazelle. When the sun comes up, you'd better be running!

We know that African American men can be disciplined, rational, responsible, organized, sober, and in complete control. So now we hear Dr. King's voice repeating the question he asked in 1968, "Where do we go from here?" The answer is clear. We must repair the damage in the community.

As Dr. Claud Anderson says in his book *Black Labor, White Wealth,* "We must adopt a strategic program (Power-nomics) to unleash Black America's potential and bring it to a level of self sufficiency and competitiveness within the next decade." During the 1960's, there were thriving independent African American records companies owned by African American men and women, like the husband and wife teams of Vivian and James Bracken who owned Vee Jay Records, in Chicago, and Sylvia and

Joe Robinson, who owned All Platinum Records in New Jersey. Two of the most successful, of course, were Berry Gordy's Motown Records in Detroit and Jim Stewart's Stax Records of Memphis, a powerhouse soul label of the mid-1960's and 1970's with a roster that included Otis Redding, Issac Hayes, Sam and Dave, Booker T and the MGs, and a young comic named Richard Pryor, to name only a few. Stewart sold Stax to Al Bell in 1970.

What was emerging was a strong African American music industry that revolved around the dominance of Soul music and the desire of entrepreneurs to own and control the African American music industry. To counter that driving ambition, the record industry began to make what they called "label deals" available to African Americans. Instead of building your own record company, a major company would create a record label for you, give you a sizable budget to operate, control the distribution of your records, and let you call yourself the CEO. What results is a so called African American record company that is actually owned by the larger parent corporation. Make no mistake, it can be a lucrative arrangement for the African American "CEO" who makes a lot of money. The consequence to African Americans is we own very few record companies.

In the Beginning Was the Word

The Million Man March created a new mindset of self-sufficiency. Barry Baszile, owner of a metal finishing plant in South Central Los Angeles, says "I would like to see more Blacks become entrepreneurs, but all of the businesses, as far as I can see, are controlled by Latinos or people from the Pacific rim. One of my missions, is to preach economic development." The message is clear, here on the eve of a brand new century. We must indeed, begin to do for self.

But it is of utmost importance to understand the various levels of the attack on African Americans. The physical level is obvious and most often we do respond to the clear aggression against African people. The torture of Haitian immigrant Abner Louima by policemen in New York's 70th Precinct provoked, among other things, A Day Of Outrage. On August 29, 1997, thousands walked peacefully across the Brooklyn Bridge and convened in front of police headquarters to demand justice. Malcolm's voice for the future cautions us about the deceit and trickery of American racism. He says that, "We are often dealing with people who are masters of Tricknology."

At one of my Agenda 2000 Leadership & Success Conferences, Dr. Na'im Akbar talked about the people in this society who attempt to dominate and oppress African

American people by getting inside our heads with self-defeating and destructive ideas. He said that these efforts are bound to succeed if we continue to cooperate with our oppressors. You participate in your own destruction if you eat what they want you to eat, read what they want you to read, listen to what they want you to listen to, and watch only what they want you to watch. In short, we must choose carefully what we allow into our lives. The words and ideas must always be healing and empowering.

CHAPTER THREE

The Balm in Gilead

Is there no balm in Gilead? Is there no physician there? Why then is not the health of the daughter of my people recovered?

Jeremiah 8:22

In addition to the ongoing aggression against the Black community, we are confronted with the consequences of decades of neglect, low performing schools, high unemployment, inadequate health care, and a litany of broken promises from African American and White political leaders. As a result, our community is engulfed in apathy.

The Black community has become the dumping ground for society's debris, from bad ideas and misinformation to toxic wastes and toxic life-styles, creating a crisis in our community as well as in our spirits. In the Chinese language, however, the word "crisis" is spelled with two characters, one representing danger, the other, opportunity. The dangers in the African American community are obvious. The opportunities, however, may not be as apparent.

The Black community is very much like an abandoned and neglected old mansion. Without vision, it appears to be nothing more than a great big beat up old house, a structure of little value. But then, there is the eye of the visionary, the one in the high ceilings and the cathedral windows. The visionary scratches the dull gray paint to reveal marble fireplaces and rosewood floors. The basic ingredients of past glory are still there. The visionary recognizes the wonderful potential of that old mansion.

There remains in the Black community much that is of value. What is required of us is the ability to see beyond the ghetto and develop that potential. The March 1996 issue of *INC. Magazine* reports the Latin wave now rising in South Los Angeles and cities across the country is part of a nationwide surge of immigrant-led economic growth. At a time when many Americans have written off urban areas as economically dead, Latinos, Asians, Arabs, and other newcomers are giving birth to a renewed, highly entrepreneurial economy that could help turn around even the most distressed neighborhoods. The article goes on to point out that, "Although Blacks have made much progress in terms of upward mobility, South Los Angeles' once bustling business corridors are either derelict or controlled by non Black entrepreneurs."

All too often we are satisfied looking back at past glories. We reminisce about the thriving Black communities of the past, the successful Black business people of the 1940's and 1950's. African American communities such as Durham, North Carolina, Tulsa, Oklahoma, and the south side of Chicago were once thriving economic enclaves. Today, Blacks are spending 97 percent of their income at non-African American businesses. Much of African American economic progress has become dependent, not on private initiatives, but on securing positions with the government or Fortune 500 corporations. Twenty-seven percent of California's African Americans are employed by the government. In comparison, only 10 percent of Latinos work for a public paycheck.

While we praise Imhotep, the African genius who designed pyramids and *wonderful* temples in his native Egypt centuries ago, we must not lose sight of the fact that here, at the dawn of a new century, we have the unique opportunity, in a real sense, to design some *wonderful* new people. To understand this challenge, it is important to understand the African concept of Sankofa. The mystical Ghanaian bird that looks backward while flying forward teaches us that it is necessary to search the past for what is valuable in order for us to move forward. It is insufficient to celebrate how great we *used* to be without designing a blueprint for the future. Our history must help create a blueprint for how great we shall be.

The Mission Statement written by Maulana Karenga and Haki Madhubuti for the Executive Council of the Million Man March is part of that blueprint.

> "Finally, we challenge each Black man, in particular, and the Black community in general to renew and expand our commitment to responsibility in personal conduct, in family relations and in obligations to the community and to the struggle for a just society and a better world. And for us to be responsible is to willingly and readily assume obligations and duties; to be accountable and dependable."

One thing is very clear: Our survival in the next century depends on African Americans developing a new sense of community, one that understands that the community is more than a physical and material place. We also exist within a social and spiritual environment.

Each community has a spirit of its own. The Million Man March Mission Statement says that one of the ways we can nourish that spirit is through reconciliation. This means we call for all of us to settle disputes, overcome conflicts, put aside grudges and hatreds in our relationships and our organizations and in the spirit of brotherhood and sisterhood; to reject and oppose communal, family, and personal violence; and to strive to build and sustain loving, mutually respectful and reciprocal relations. In a word, to seek the good, find it, embrace it, and build on it.

To understand and appreciate the value of New York State Regent Adelaide Sanford as a member of the community is quite different from being awed or impressed by the flashing drug dealer or "living large" entertainer, who may also have a presence in the community. To appreciate a loving and committed educator like Dr. Sanford is to operate from a family-centered value system that seeks to nourish the very spirit of the people. To be impressed by the flashy life-style is to operate from a value system that rewards material gains with little regard for what happens on the street where the community spirit suffers the consequences.

Our behavior must nourish community spirit. The

energy that resonates in the community must bond us in harmony and respect. This new vibration, while it will operate in the larger community, can begin in your home. Control the language in your home. Speak with love and respect. Don't allow offensive terms and foul language. You can even control the aromas, the mood, and the music that fill your home. We enhance the psyche of the community by starting on an individual level.

We learned a lot about the strength of community when Ron Daniels, the Director of the Center for Constitutional Rights, led a fact finding delegation to Haiti in 1995. What they found was a people with a strong spirit of community, despite their poverty. Even though they were reeling from decades of oppression, they had a powerful sense of self-determination. They were clear about their identity and their culture. They understood that above all else, they deserved to be free. It was the triumphant spirit of the people that held them together, and that same spirit is evident in the historical experiences of African Americans.

Stephanie Shaw, in her book on Black professional women during the Jim Crow era in America, describes a typical African American community in 1912. She points out that the community in this instance was more than a neighborhood. Interest, rather than buildings and borders, determined membership. Composed dynamically of a diverse group of people, it was a social institution or an arrangement of people who possessed a common understanding of history. The community was in fact held together by mutual interest in the present and shared visions of the future for the group and all its members.

Our challenge is to renew that spirit. If we fail to build and sustain the Black family and community we betray the legacy and the traditions of our ancestors. The leadership in the 21st century will come from the visionaries who can see beyond physical circumstances to what can be. One of the things I noticed on NIGHTTALK was how often callers would correctly analyze the political or social condition of the Black community. I began to call it the "hip analysis." There were many people who were very pleased with their astute or "hip analysis" and felt the analysis alone was sufficient to strike a blow against oppression. As a result, no further action on their part would be necessary. They had participated in the liberation struggle of African American people simply by calling the talk show. We must resist the temptation to be satisfied with correctly explaining or interpreting the current reality. I realize now that all of the voices I have been hearing over the years have been urging us to create a new reality, one that comes from a newer sense of how we build, how we create, and how we solve problems.

We must learn to make the distinction between change and exchange. For instance, to place homeless people in a shelter exchange one circumstance for another without changing the fundamental condition of the people. Lack of shelter is not why people are homeless. The absence of jobs and the lack of skills training, quality education, and affordable housing are the fundamental causes of homelessness. So it is in these areas that we can effectively change the conditions of homeless people. We can empower them to provide and maintain homes for themselves. In short, new constructs will have to be developed. We will have to alter our concepts of change. But as a starting point, the change must be internal.

Black folks are often asked and indeed, we often ask ourselves, how is it that other ethnic groups, some of whom have been in America for a relatively short period of time, are able to make more progress than African Americans? We have been struggling for power and greater control of our own destiny ever since our arrival on these shores.

Most often the Jewish community is pointed to, since Jewish immigrants who began arriving in America in the early days of the 20th century encountered a particularly hostile social and political environment similar to the condition African Americans face even to this day. The comparisons have continued with the arrival of the Koreans, Indians, Chinese, and Arabs during the 1980's and 90's. The fact is, these groups have done quite well. The Jewish community is stable and largely self-sufficient. They own banks, television and radio stations, newspapers, hospitals, schools, housing developments, resorts, and much more. They are major players in a number of industries.

Asian and East Indian entrepreneurs are prevalent in many small businesses, most seem to exist in the Black community. Most interesting is the presence of Asians in the African American hair care industry. This is an industry that depends entirely on Black consumer dollars. However, the manufacturing, distributing, and retailing of African American hair care products are dominated by Whites and Asians. Few Blacks own beauty supply stores. Asians own the great majority of nail salons in the African American community. The twenty-one Black hair care manufacturers which constitute the African American Beauty Aids Institute with the queen on the product are desperately trying to maintain a respectable market share.

New York is a city of immigrants, most recently from the Caribbean and Pacific Rim. In fact, during the 1980's, some 280,000 Asians arrived in New York City. Rather than remain in low-income ghettos, these groups pool their resources and work together to achieve their economic goals. More than any other group, Asians represent New York's emerging middle class.

Among Asian Americans, a priority is placed on education, ownership, and family and not necessarily in that order. Seventy-eight percent of all Asians live in married couple households. The divorce rate is low and most Asians marry other Asians. Entrepreneurship is a priority for Asians, especially Koreans, who not only have the highest self-employment rate among Asians, but the highest business ownership rate of any ethnic or racial group including Whites. Some Asians project that by the year 2000, 75 percent of Californians will be working for an Asian-owned business or paying rent to an Asian landlord.

How then do we explain the differences in the fortunes of African Americans and that of other groups who also face American racism and resistance? One factor of course is obvious: None of these groups have been confronted with the same level or type of aggression as African Americans. Dr. Claud Anderson of the Harvest Institute points out, African Americans have been socially engineered toward underclass status by a public policy that has operated from the slave codes to the Black codes, from Jim Crow laws to institutional racism.

However, another significant question remains. How indeed did these other groups avoid the consequences of American racism? Anti-Semitism was and remains deadly. There is a wave of anti-immigrant sentiment sweeping America. This is evident in everything from "English only" legislation to California's Proposition 187 and 209 that limits immigration and affirmative action. But this anti-immigrant sentiment is not new. It is rooted in the history of America, a nation made up primarily of European immigrants who have always felt compelled to dominate and control all others on these shores. So how did these other groups manage to circumvent white supremacy? How is it that they were not trapped and contained by the racism that is truly as American as apple pie? The answer lies in how each group has responded to America. And it is of critical importance to understand what distinguishes the African American response from all the rest.

Each ethnic group arriving in America (perhaps with a clearer understanding of America than the Africans who were forcibly brought here and raised in servitude and repression) set out to *protect* themselves from America, while African Americans set out to *change* America. Joel Kotkin, author of *Tribes,* points out that other groups use their race, religion, and cultural identity to knit them together and determine their success. For Blacks, race, religion, and cultural identity is submerged as we struggle to transform the heart of America by convincing White Americans that we are all the same and that America's future depends on the country's willingness to cut us in and share the fruits of the American dream. In fact, the dream of an America where all people are judged by the content of their character is the only part of Dr. King's August 1964 speech that is exalted. The main body of the speech that spoke to social and economic justice is all but ignored.

Other ethnic groups embraced strategies based on what America really is, rather than what the country might one day become. These groups—the Jews of the early 20th century and their descendants, as well as the Asians,

Arabs, and the Indians of the late 20th century—transformed America with self-reliance. They would turn to each other first, pool their resources and count on each other to achieve their economic and social goals. They would not wait to be included in the mainstream. Instead, they would work to create and control smaller economic streams of their own. They avoided racism in hiring by owning businesses. They defeated red lining in the banking industry by owning banks.

Today, in New York City's crowded Chinatown, the Chinese have some 28 banks; there were only six in the 1970's. In an even shorter amount of time, 31 banks have opened to serve the strong Korean population of Flushing, Queens. By 1988, there were some 600 garment factories in Chinatown with payrolls of $200 million. The Chinese avoided job discrimination by creating jobs for themselves. Joel Kotkin points out that this ethos of self-help, with all of its occasional flaws and excesses, characterizes virtually all of the groups ascending in America and globally as well.

African Americans must also embrace our culture and aggressively embrace each other in order to change our condition in America. We must protect our existence in America. We must operate from positions of strength, economically and politically. The voice of Marcus Garvey calling for self-sufficiency remains pertinent for the future!

The increasing move toward Black economic development fueled by African American dollars is essential. As Rev. June Gatlin says, "Hold onto and handle what we have more intelligently and therefore more efficiently." We must continue to create and control our own industries, particularly the hair care and music industries. We are the only consumers in the former and the largest in the latter. We must manufacture, distribute, and retail. Ken Smikle, publisher of *Target Market News,* reports, "African Americans are major consumers of many products and determine the bottom line for many companies."

Black households continue to spend more dollars on average than White households for food items, fruit flavored drinks, sugar, seasonings, apparel items, automobiles, liquor, cigarettes, snacks, color TV's, and telephone service. However, little of this spending is done within African American businesses. Instead, this spending represents a drain on the Black community and a blessing for all other communities. African Americans need to rethink how we use and determine the value of our consumer dollars. Every dollar we spend has the power to create employment opportunities for Blacks.

How we choose to spend $500 billion is the most important decision we can make on behalf of our economic empowerment. Earl Graves publisher of Black Enterprise offers the following illustration in his September 1996 editorial.

> "Let's say you just bought a new suit for work, and you paid $450. You are happy with the price and the quality of your purchase. You found the suit at a convenient location and the customer service was superb. Did you get a good deal? Maybe so, or maybe not. Now here's my idea of a great deal. Let's say I bought the same suit for the same price. I saw the suit in an ad in my favorite African American magazine; at the store where I bought the suit, there were African American sales managers. The company that designed and manufactured the suit is African American-owned, or at least has African Americans in senior management and on its board of directors. The manufacturer of the suit does business with African American companies, ranging from its public relations firm to the investment bank that helped raise expansion capital. Finally, because of a special promotion, five percent of the retail price of my suit will be donated to the United Negro College Fund."

Graves calls this Reciprocal Benefit Premiums (RBPs). You made sure that at least some of your $450 would re-circulate to other African Americans in the form of education, employment, and business revenues. The bottom line is, we must maximize the economic influence we wield as consumers. Each and every purchase we make can be a contribution to African American empowerment. That is real power, but only if *we choose to use* it.

We must begin to make informed rational decisions that empower us as a people rather than led by impulsive consumption that empowers other groups. We must choose behaviors that will move African American people away from the brink of disaster, where we are assigned the status of a permanent underclass, and begin to move instead toward a new level of self sufficiency, using the financial and intellectual resources that already exist in the African American family and community.

There have been many discussions on NIGHTTALK about the self-help ethic that existed among Blacks at the turn of the century. Many callers to the show have recalled with pride African American communities like the Pitts Hill district in Pittsburgh, Sweet Auburn in Atlanta, Black Wall Street in Tulsa, all thriving African American communities with banks, insurance companies, and diverse businesses that produced African American millionaires, like A.C. Gatson and Madam C.J. Walker. Recently, we have begun to celebrate the history of the old Negro Baseball League. The self-help ethic was thought to be evident there as well in that many teams and stadiums were owned by prosperous Black men and women.

Part of the frustration expressed by the voices I have heard throughout the years has been based on our failure as an African American community to adopt those same principles of self-reliance that our foreparents seemed to understand so well. However, I am suggesting that the failure to pass along this self-help ethic is because it never was institutionalized. Clearly, there were individuals like Marcus Garvey who taught self reliance, but it was not institutionalized. The thriving Black communities of the 1930's and 1940's did not exist so much out of *self-reliance* but *self-defense*.

Blacks who could not eat in White restaurants or sleep in White hotels, had little choice but to build their own. If they could not play in the "white major leagues," it would be necessary to have a league of their own. If the White insurance company would not insure African Americans, then a Black insurance company was the only alternative. The fact is, Blacks had no choice. It was do for self, or do without!

It was not the hostile reaction by Whites to the success of Blacks that destroyed thriving African American communities. It was not the violence against these communities, no more than lynchings, assassinations, and fire bombings could ever destroy the Black movement for freedom and justice in America. What was thought to be a powerful self-help ethic was easily destroyed, however, by a new choice, a choice that came disguised as *integration*. Now, given a choice—a White hotel or a Black hotel, White restaurant or a Black restaurant, White college or Black college, or a White baseball team with one Black man on it or the Negro League—Black Folks chose the White over its Black counterpart every time, until Black establishments no longer existed.

Of course, what occurred in America was desegregation, not integration. Blacks abandoned their own and began to spend freely in White-owned establishments, but Whites never ventured away from their own, not even for a moment. They continued to spend their dollars among themselves.

The quality of life in the African American community will dramatically improve when we choose to mobilize our political, intellectual, and economic power to build and sustain the Black community through the recreation of independent African American institutions that address our needs. Our challenge as Blacks is to recognize the best of our culture, heritage, and traditions, and begin to use them to rebuild and sustain our communities. But we need not stop at what has been passed down from previous generations. We must also use the intellectual capital of more recent generations. The work of Maulana Karenga, not the least of which are the principles of Kwanzaa is of great value. The insights and institution building of Haki Madhubuti and Jawanza Kunjufu are of significant importance. Kunjufu's *Countering the Conspiracy to Destroy Black Boys* is a valuable blueprint for African American parents. This and many other works are rooted in an awareness of contemporary reality. They document the changes that have occurred in American society, particularly the way in which white supremacy, has been maintained throughout this century.

African Americans are a powerful and resourceful people. When we consider that there has been insufficient improvement in the psychological, economic, and political status of the masses of Black people, it is clear that the resources of the Black community must finally be used by that community to move African Americans to a new level of self-sufficiency.

Voices for the Future

There is a balm in Gilead to make the wounded whole. God has already blessed us with tools, talent, training, and even money. All the voices I have heard proclaim that there is a balm in Black America to heal the soul, again. Adam Clayton Powell, Jr. asked what is still an important question, "What's in your hand, Black man?" Here in this final decade of the 20th century, just look at what is already in our hands.

CHAPTER FOUR

From Prominence to Power

"All organized societies depend on a power system; and politics is the business of power, its acquisition and its use."
                                         Michael Manley

All too often, African Americans are encouraged to support Black faces in high places. Entertainers, athletes, political appointees, and a litany of prominent Blacks in corporate America are often lifted as symbols of progress and success for the entire group.

We are encouraged to celebrate *prominent* Blacks rather than *powerful* African Americans, and we are repeatedly given empty symbols as a substitute for real progress. Too many people with titles have little or no effect on the overall quality of life in the Black community. There is a difference between prominence and power. While prominent people often have power, it is also possible to have prominence and no real power at all. When a prominent Black businessman decided to enter into a joint venture with Minister Farrakhan and supply the containers for the Nation of Islam's Clean & Fresh soap products, Whites opposed to Farrakhan objected, and the Black businessman withdrew, fearing the loss of the support of those Whites upon whom his business depended.

The mainstream political arena, as well as much of corporate America, illustrates this concern. Currently, Blacks have great visibility in major corporations as executives and board members. African Americans were showcased at both the Democratic and Republican conventions. The GOP even allowed J.C. Watts, a Black conservative, to respond to President Clinton's State of the Nation speech. He echoed the party line and engaged in only name calling African American leaders. Blacks are prominent, however, given the policies enacted by both parties, they have little influence in the corridors of power. One of the most prominent Republicans in America is General Colin Powell, but the Republican party remains particularly hostile to African Americans.

Bill Clinton's visible Black advisors and cabinet

level staffers have very little power. They could not change the President's appalling decision on the Crime Bill and Welfare Reform, nor could they convince him to soundly condemn the firebombing of Black churches that occurred in the South during his first term in office. Nonetheless, African Americans are expected to point with pride to the prominent African Americans in the political and corporate arena. In fact many Blacks accept these symbols of individual achievement as indicative of the entire group's progress, while other groups get results.

The Black community of Brooklyn has 15 African American elected officials, yet the Metro Tech development project in downtown Brooklyn, a multimillion dollar project that includes the construction of office towers, retail stores, luxury housing, and Brooklyn's only major hotel, ends across the street from where the Black community begins. The presence and prominence of African American politicians need not produce power for Black communities; it seems that having African Americans in office is adequate.

As the quality of public education continues to decline, unemployment rates rise, hospitals close, and living conditions erode, African Americans are offered slogans and symbols instead of real progress. Some are satisfied perhaps because the slogans are, in fact, empowering. It is a good idea to "keep your eyes on the prize" and to "keep hope alive." However, the voices for the future remind us that we cannot allow slogans and symbols to become substitutes for substance. Whether on a political or personal level, we must recognize what is meaningful and of real value in our lives. There must be a redistribution of wealth in this country. Money and training must be made available by both private and public sectors. African Americans must leverage their 500 billion dollars in the private sector and our almost twenty million votes in the public sector. Presently the private and public sector don't respect us and feel we will be satisfied with positions of prominence.

Moderate Black leaders continue, however, to suggest that pragmatism, both personally and politically, will achieve our goals, however limited. Pragmatism requires that we do not offend Whites whom, we are told, we must ultimately depend on for our own successes. Michael Manley, Jamaica's Prime Minister, challenged this notion of pragmatism when he said,

> "When one considers the magnitude of the economic and attitudinal restructuring which our condition demands, it becomes clear that the politics of conservatism and tinkering are not only irrelevant to our situation, but represent an intolerable default of responsibility."

In pressing for alliances with other groups, New York Congressman Major Owens of Brooklyn's Black 11th Congressional District has, on occasion, told African American audiences "that Black people could not ever expect to accomplish anything on their own." African Americans are all too often urged to wait until someone else is able to help us with our problems. White power brokers are comforted by the so-called pragmatism of moderate African American leaders and their basic agreement with the existing social framework. Moderate Black leaders believe that only marginal adjustments are needed to relieve discontent and at the same time make the existing system more efficient. Thus, they avoid making the significant changes that many Whites still find are threatening.

For old line Black leaders, the idea of African Americans devising and implementing our own strategies is frightening or perceived as impossible. A new mindset is needed, one that will release us from the psychology of dependence. This will be traumatic. Black Mayors like Goode of Philadelphia and Dinkins of New York were more concerned about not offending the White electorate than empowering African Americans who voted them in office. They were compelled to put some distance between themselves and their own communities in order to reassure Whites that they could be trusted. No White mayor has ever been required to reassure the Black community about anything.

There is an effort to invent ideal and acceptable Blacks as models for what all African Americans should be. One of the favorite ploys used to confuse African Americans is the projection of the ideal Black man, someone who succeeds in spite of the social and political realities in American society. Most recently, General Colin Powell was lifted as the ideal Black man. His is a success story with which most Whites feel comfortable. Powell, we are told, achieved success because his priorities were correct. He was not angry or bitter at America for its treatment of African Americans. In fact, he was projected as a loyal American whose African heritage was quite unimportant to him throughout most of his life and career. At least that is how he was projected to the African American community. In his book, *My American Journey*, General Powell says that it was not until he visited Africa as an adult that he realized he was African.

The more insidious subterfuge, however, is in the use of Powell as well and others as models for Black success. Colin Powell, we are told, is successful because he refused to let racism get in his way. In other words, American society requires that Powell makes peace with racism rather than require that Whites eliminate it.

An effective way to make the aggression against African American people invisible is to ignore the behavior of the aggressor and focus on our responses. It is when the victim accepts the challenge to simply circumvent oppression, and when we are silent in the face of racist attacks on African American people that we subtly give permission to others to continue the injustice. The fact that we are not looking to others to do for us does not mean that we ignore their behavior and tolerate injustice. While it is necessary to avoid the victims' syndrome, we must also understand that you do not improve your condition by pretending that you are no longer a victim.

Optimism and seeing yourself as a winner is of value; however, there is an important distinction to be made between being victimized and being defeated. While you may admit you are a victim of racism, thus acknowledging the barriers and social engineering that affect our lives, it does not follow that you accept defeat. To acknowledge that you are under attack is a necessary prerequisite to creating a plan for fighting back.

African Americans must not be confused. When we say "racism is a fact of life" or "racism will always be there so why focus on it," we are inadvertently allowing oppression to become normalized. As a starting point for achieving our goals, we must first create the mindset necessary for success. One such mindset is understanding that we need not tolerate injustice.

In a NIGHTTALK interview, Rachel Robinson, the wife of baseball great Jackie Robinson, said that one of the things her husband's experience taught them was that if a Black man is as aggressive as he should be, he will be considered hostile. The legendary Billy Eckstine was often called a hard-nosed no-nonsense guy. He said he never saw himself that way, he just believed in insisting on what he was entitled to. Part of the fire that powered both these legends, Robinson and Eckstine, to success were the clear understanding that their aspirations were legitimate and that they were entitled to go as far as their talent could take them. But there was also the realization that they had the right to remove whatever obstacles they found in their way. Clearly, these were men who refused to be twice as good only to be considered equal. They insisted on being recognized for what they truly accomplished. They would not be satisfied with less than they deserved.

Secondly, we must think clearly and identify those things that are truly meaningful. In my interviews with the leaders of the major civil rights organizations, they invariably point to fiscal status and reputation as measures of their organizations' viability and effectiveness. During the movement of the 1960's, the leaders of these same organizations would point instead to the ways they were effectively challenging injustice. Most often in debt, behind in their bills, staff unpaid, and the rent due. SNCC (Student Nonviolent Coordinating Committee) and CORE (Congress Of Racial Equality) staffers remember that during the height of the struggle, paychecks were rare. Fiscal viability was not their primary concern. The measure of the success of these organizations was how often and how effectively they could strike a blow against oppression.

These were the organizations that effectively changed the social landscape of this country. Today, the drum majors for justice have been replaced by corporate bureaucrats. While fiscal stability is desirable, there must be a balance. We cannot sacrifice our commitment to social and economic justice in return for Dun & Bradstreet approval. The elimination of bigotry and tyranny will not occur from a good credit rating. A sound fiscal strategy must be a sister to a sound political strategy. At this point, there is still no balance.

Today's civil rights leadership asks to be held in high regard because of corporate America's confidence in them. The Black community is expected to appreciate these prominent African American leaders even though problems previously cited continue to plague our communities. Most have not even spoken about the need for a new trial for Mumia Abu-Jamal, who is imprisoned in Pennsylvania.

We keep trading power for prominence. When African Americans become powerful, systems change, and that is threatening to White supremacists. When Kwame Toure, then known as Stokely Carmichael, first shouted "Black power" in 1968, Dr. King and other Black leaders felt uncomfortable with the term and rushed to reassure Whites that Stokely didn't mean any harm. Most Whites are threatened by Black power because they have been guilty of abuses of power.

Independent Black initiatives are criticized and discouraged for being divisive. In New York City, when I organized Recycle Black Dollars campaigns, Mayor Giuliani learned of the efforts to encourage African American consumers to support Black businesses and decided to protest this initiative on the part of African Americans, by going to 125th Street, Harlem's main shopping district, to shop only at white owned stores. Instead, he attempted to depict the self-help strategy of Blacks as inappropriate behavior, as did two White women, who picketed the Black World Book Store in Detroit, whose owners had publicly criticized the African American author, Terry McMillan, who they said, only did book signings at white owned book stores while she was in Detroit. The White women said it was inappropriate and even racist for the Black store to expect support from an African American author. While at the same time, similar efforts on the part of other groups are lifted as examples of an honorable work ethic and boot strap success. We are given examples of Chinatown, Koreantown, Greektown, Jewtown, and Little Italy. African Americans however, must operate in alliance with other groups, or be accused of reverse racism.

It is of course of the utmost importance to fully develop individual skill. In spite of all the excellent work by Black writers and motivators instructing African Americans on the value of tapping into our inner powers these strategies for personal development are usually given without any connection to the development of the larger community as a whole. When you consider the very real political and social realities affecting the lives of African Americans, it is absolutely clear that Blacks cannot afford to be Black and ignorant at the same time. We cannot afford to be Black and unprepared to meet the challenges of the new millennium. The real value of our skills and talents is when they serve group progress. African Americans like to say that we are not monolithic. We talk about how diverse we are (with great pride), but, our strength comes from our common understanding of history. Our strength comes from recognizing our mutual interests. Our strength also comes from our shared visions of the future. Our strength comes from what we have in common and not from our cherished diversity.

Michael Jordan and Scottie Pippen have excellent individual skills, but the real value of their talents is demonstrated when they contribute to the team effort. The Bulls won six NBA championships because of team effort. The same thing is true of Asian business people. It is not their sole intention to achieve individual success. In fact, their personal success is often measured by how well their efforts improved the condition of the entire group. In his book, *Tribes*, Joel Kotkin examines how race, religion, and identity determine success. When Jews began to achieve a greater measure of economic power, they were not loath to use it for the protection of even the most distant branches of the tribe.

> "As Jews began their first mass migrations from Russia, the tradition of self-help brought critical assistance to newcomers from the already established communities, particularly in Britain, France, Germany, and the United States. In 1914, there were over 514 different Jewish benevolent societies in the United States alone, providing everything from insurance and burial plots to summer camps for children."

When we "do for self," as many Blacks are fond of saying, it is important to be clear of our intentions. Self-reliance is not selfishness or separatist. Self-reliance is the recognition that each of us is responsible for controlling our own destinies and carving out a future for our families and our community. Considering the social realities challenging African Americans, self-reliance must include a willingness to work toward the welfare of the entire group. As we need power to shape our lives, it is quite legitimate for Blacks to organize around the acquisition and use of power.

Dr. King's voice for the future reminds us that,

From Prominence to Power

> The tendencies to ignore the Negroís contributions to American life and to strip him of his personhood is as old as the earliest history book and as contemporary as the morningís newspapers. As long as the mind is enslaved the body can never be free. No Emancipation Proclamation, no civil rights bill can totally bring this kind of freedom. The Negro will only be free when he reaches down to the inner depths of his own being and signs with a pen and ink of assertive manhood his own emancipation proclamation. Another basic challenge is to discover how to organize our strengths into economic and political power. No one can deny that the Negro is in dire need of this kind of legitimate power.

The problem with transforming the ghetto, therefore, is a problem of power. There will be a confrontation between the forces of power demanding change and the forces of power dedicated to the preserving of the status quo. Now power properly understood is nothing but the ability to achieve a purpose.

Currently, the level of political consciousness among far too many Black politicians is dangerously low Consider the Congressional Black Caucus, whose members rarely show unity. Their votes are often conflicting. Some of them voted for the Clinton Crime Bill in an effort to support Democratic Party unity, while others voted their conscience and opposed the bill. Some voted for the Communications Act, even though it prevents African American ownership of radio stations. When the Caucus was advised by the National Association of Black Owned Broadcasters of the harmful effect the legislation would have on small independent African American owners, many Black Congressmen shrugged off their yes votes by saying they did not understand what they were supporting. The significance of having a Black Caucus is for them to leverage their power and vote as a bloc even when there are differences. This is the dismal state of Black leadership.

On another occasion, Congressman John Conyers of Detroit, in cooperation with the Center for Constitutional Rights, convened hearings on police violence in New York City, a city where reports of violence by the police have increased steadily since the election of Rudolph Giuliani as Mayor. One of the most glaring examples was the alleged beating and torture of Abner Louima, a Haitian immigrant. Louima said he was brutalized by New York City policemen who repeatedly thrust a plunger into his rectum, causing severe and life threatening damage to his internal organs. It was further alleged that while the torture was going on, one of his police tormentors proclaimed "this is Giuliani time," a reference to the different atmosphere on the police department since Giuliani replaced the city's first African American Mayor, David Dinkins.

When Conyers convened the hearings, most of New York's African American elected officials ignored them. They followed the lead of Mayor Giuliani, who denounced the hearings and called them unnecessary. The day-long event in which hundreds of witnesses testified before members of the House Judiciary Committee, a panel which included Congresswoman Sheila Jackson Lee from Houston and Congressman Donald Payne from Newark, as well as other members of the New York Delegation, including Rep. Nydia Velazquez and Rep. Jose Serrano. In fact, the hearings were paid for by the Judiciary Committee and were considered a Congressional session. Nonetheless, Rep. Charles Rangel dismissed them as nothing more than a Rep. Major Owens political rally and refused to attend, saying that it was not an official hearing. What was seemingly lost to the Black politicians was that to their constituents who were looking for a way to stop police violence, the hearings were quite official.

These public hearings also came at a time when President Clinton was calling for a dialogue on racism in America. The victims of police violence are primarily Black and Latino, and thus the White press has overlooked the problem. Congressman Conyer's hearings were an effort to force this awful reality into public view where it could be confronted. African American politicians who were given a significant opportunity to move on behalf of their people engaged instead in petty, party politics, and as usual, went off in various conflicting directions.

I hear Black people around the country express their feelings of having been betrayed by many African American leaders and politicians. At the core of this leadership dilemma is a profound sense of confusion as to what we should be demanding of our leaders. That confusion was addressed momentarily at the 1997 NAACP National Convention in Pittsburgh when the delegates wanted to discuss the future direction of the NAACP. Should the NAACP remain focused primarily on integration, or should it shift to a new national thrust for self-reliance?

The NAACP and many African American leaders continue to pursue liberation through integration and Black progress through dependency on White people. As a result, measures that African Americans embrace and that Whites find offensive, like the Recycle Black Dollars Campaign in which African Americans are urged to patronize Black businesses, are most often rejected or minimized by mainstream African American leaders who do not want to offend Whites.

Fortunately, there is a model for independent leadership. On October 20, 1972, a year before his death, Amilcar Cabral, Secretary General of the Africa Party for the Independence of Guinea and the Cape Verde Islands, gave us a voice for the future when he told a group of African Americans, "Any movement for freedom must be based on the concrete realities of those people. Today's fight is a continuation of the fight to defend our dignity and our right to have our own identity."

Kwame Nkrumah's voice for the future said, "We have before us not only an opportunity, but an historic duty. It is in our hands to join our strength, taking sustenance from our diversity, honoring our rich and varied traditions and culture, but acting together for the protection and benefit of us all."

The importance of self-reliance and group unity that moves to the need of one's own people first is a necessity. Part of the dilemma facing Black leadership is the failure to agree on the primary needs and interests of their constituents. It is absolutely necessary that leaders understand the context of our time. The role of African American leaders and politicians must be constantly upgraded and renewed to fit within the context of a constantly changing reality. It seems that many are in a time warp, expecting the strategies of the past to remain relevant forever.

New leadership will have to go beyond the timid, pragmatic leadership style that disguises itself in cowardly opportunism. There is a need to return to the principled leadership of Fannie Lou Hamer and Medger Evers. Those leaders fought for issues their people valued. Mainstream Black leaders have sought the liberation of African American people within the limits set by the oppressive forces they are charged to fight against. They are unable to acknowledge that the long-range interests of Blacks and Whites do not necessarily coincide. It is unlikely that Whites are willing to pay for or even aid in the building of strong independent African American communities. In short, Blacks will very likely have to build and support our own institutions in America, Africa, and the Caribbean. W.E.B. DuBois' voice for the future said, "Race loyalty need never become hatred of other people or envy of their success, but rather an unending self sacrificing desire for excellence." Whites seem to fear and resent the creation of independent Black institutions organized to meet the needs of African Americans.

As long as Whites see these simple acts of self-reliance as seditious, it will remain difficult to form the kind of alliance with them that would truly benefit Blacks. New Black leaders should refuse to trade off the legitimate goals and aspirations for the total liberation of African Americans in order to accommodate the fears of Whites. Black leadership will have to be committed to the needs of African Americans first.

In the Black community there is the very clear need to harness economic and political power to reverse the declining status of the community. It must be clear by now that Black faces in high places are certainly insufficient. Marcus Garvey's prophetic voice for the future said, "Action, self-reliance, the vision of self, and the future have been the only means by which the oppressed have seen and realized the light of their own freedom."

CHAPTER FIVE

Africentricity to the Rescue

"What is the truth? Or more precisely, who's truth shall we express, that of the oppressed, or that of the oppressor?"

Larry Neal

As a result of an increasing awareness and appreciation of their African heritage, many African Americans have begun to research and study African history. There is, in fact, a cultural renaissance sweeping the African American community, which acknowledges the contributions of our African ancestors. However, what often occurs is only a celebration of our greatness, but our history also offers an opportunity to reflect on past mistakes. Our understanding of history will determine the course of our future actions. How should we see history? What should we feel about it? What are the very real lessons of history? The answers to these questions are important because they will determine whether we move into the future feeling empowered or confused.

John Hope Franklin, one of America's preeminent historians and a noted authority on the African American experience, gives us a voice for the future by saying, "Knowledge of our history is crucial to Black America's future." The old stories are relevant and are important landmarks on our blueprint for the future. African Americans must not escape the harsh present by returning to a glorious African past, but be inspired and empowered by that history. It is important that we understand the principle of Sankofa, a word from the Akan people of West Africa that means we must return back and recapture our past in order to move forward.

Poet and activist Larry Neal once pointed out that what separated a Malcolm X from a Roy Wilkins was a profound difference in how each man understood American history. The same is true today. The tension between the major civil rights groups and the masses of African American people is rooted in how the leadership of these groups understands and expresses the emotional realities of African Americans.

For instance, the leaders who organized the Million Man March interpreted and felt the history of African

American people differently from the moderate leaders of the civil rights organizations. The March leaders were more in touch with the masses than the civil rights leaders were even capable of being. History impacts on all generations, and each generation of African Americans has a need to understand the challenges of their history. As Marcus Garvey's voice for the future said, "Black men, you were once great, you shall be great again. Lose not courage, lose not faith, go forward." Past greatness teaches us that we are capable of great things in the future.

During the organizing of the Million Man March, Minister Farrakhan, Benjamin Muhammed, then known as Reverend Ben Chavis, and I taped a local TV show called The McCreary Report for New York's Channel 5. That was followed later that evening by a mass rally, hosted by Reverend Calvin Butts, at Harlem's historic Abyssinian Baptist Church. As we waited before taping the TV show and in Dr. Butts' office before the rally, we talked of how confident we felt that the community would embrace the idea of a million African American men gathering in Washington, DC. There was no doubt in our minds that African American men would respond. If indeed our ancestors were great and courageous people whose ambition led to great historical accomplishments, how could we, their descendants, call for anything less than the largest demonstration of Black unity ever organized in this country. Our sense of history demanded, as Garvey said, "That we lose not faith and go forward."

The aggression against African Americans operates on many levels. One of the most sinister aspects of that aggression is the effort to normalize the concepts of white supremacy by exalting European thoughts and ideas. At the same time Africentricity is attacked as mere ethnic cheerleading, which implies that all claims of African achievement are false and misleading.

However, decades of European philosophical domination came to a dramatic end with the dawn of the 1990's. Even though many Black scholars have always resisted the constructs of white supremacy, the 1990's saw the demand for new curricula inclusive of African history sweep the nation. Two of those curricula were the Portland Baseline Essays and SETCLAE produced by African American Images. I organized parents and students to file a class action lawsuit against the New York City Board of Education in July of 1990. The lawsuit and the community activism which accompanied it challenged many ideas that have been used against African Americans and other people of color. The lawsuit asked that the New

York City Board of Education rewrite and update all curricula. The centerpiece of any new curricula would be to accurately portray Africans throughout the diaspora.

Intellectual inferiority and the so-called failure of Black family life are two ideas that have been used to denigrate Black people. The implication is that when Black children fail in school, it is either because of genetics or because they do not come from good families. These oversimplifications tend to ignore the social and political realities that influence psychological development and shape the physical environment that controls the lives of young people. White-only curricula, low teacher expectations, tracking, a misunderstanding of African American children's learning styles, and an outright contempt for Black students must also be considered. I believe some school failures are so harmful and deep seated that the time is past for marginal tinkering within the existing educational system. It is time to take action. We must stop blaming the victim and acknowledge that schools are the major culprits for students' failures.

Still, there is the ongoing effort to absolve the schools of their fundamental responsibility to educate all children regardless of their social condition. *Visions of a Better Way: A Black Appraisal of Public Schooling*, a report issued by the Joint Center for Political Studies in Washington, DC, states that "we must demand that the schools shift their focus from the supposed deficiencies of the Black child and the alleged inadequacies of Black family life and confront instead the barriers that stand in the way of academic success."

That current Eurocentric curriculum of distortion and misinformation is still widely being used by public schools nationwide is a major problem. In spite of a sustained effort to trivialize and even demonize Africentrism, there continues to be a growing national movement to infuse African American contributions into the larger curricula. The entire subject of history needs to be rewritten to include the African presence. How can history be taught without an accurate understanding of the first people on earth?

The Oakland, California, school board ignited a firestorm of controversy when they proposed a bilingual program that would help teachers understand Ebonics. They felt it would enhance teachers' ability to help children "code switch" their thoughts into "standard English." Ebonics is a linguistic style firmly rooted in the lives and minds of the Black community. Rather than denigrate students for speaking Ebonics, use it as a tool to translate into standard English. Rather than dismiss this linguistic

Africentricity to the Rescue

style as ignorant and backward, the Oakland school board recognized the social conditions that gave rise to this linguistic style.

By declaring Ebonics a language, the Oakland school board had subtly challenged the notion of white supremacy. The detractors argued that the school board was proposing to teach Ebonics instead of standard English, even though from the outset the board had been clear that this was not their intention. They wanted to use the same technique that is used to teach newly arrived immigrants proficiency in reading and writing standard English. There is money for bilingual education, but it is not available to Black students since according to the current Eurocentric standard, there is no second language to teach. Most Whites and prominent African Americans were threatened by the audacity of the Oakland school board's acknowledgment of African speech patterns and linguistic styles as legitimate. The Ebonics debate demonstrated that European concepts are not the only valid ideas in the universe.

Africentricity is not intended as an attack on Whites, but an appreciation of multiculturalism with Africa as the point of origin and frame of reference.

However, as the presence and accomplishments of other cultures are affirmed, the precepts of European philosophical dominance begin to fade. It should be pointed out that not all Whites are threatened by this resurgence of the truth. When I interviewed Jack Weatherford, on NIGHTTALK, a White anthropologist and author of *Indian Givers: How the Indians of the Americas Transformed the World*, he acknowledged the long denied contributions of Native Americans including food and medicine. Native Americans discovered the first effective treatment for malaria, and their democratic style of government provided the model upon which this country was designed. When you consider how much the European settlers took from the Native populations in terms of food, medicine, and ideas, as well as land and human lives, it becomes clear that Europeans did not discover America, they invaded it. Henry Loren Katz, another White author, has also documented the achievements of Africans and Native Americans in the United States.

Africentricity is not a distortion of history contrived by Africans and African Americans hoping to construct a wonderful mythical past. It is a movement that is powered by the pursuit of the truth, and many scholars of various ethnicities have been involved. In his book *Black*

Africentricity to the Rescue

Athena, Martin Bernal (a respected White historian) challenges popular thinking about "classical civilization." He argues that civilization has deep roots in Afro Asiatic cultures, but these influences have been systematically ignored, denied, or suppressed since the 18th century, chiefly for racist reasons! Bernal notes that it will be necessary to rethink the fundamental basis of Western civilization, but first we must understand how racism has influenced histography and philosophy.

The point is that African Americans are entitled to a fuller understanding of history that is free from European biases. Barbara Solow, of Harvard's W.E.B. DuBois Institute for Afro American Research says, "We study African American history not to assuage White guilt, or to engender Black pride, but to replace racist myths with a truer understanding of history." In order to reject all notions of race supremacy, we must learn to recognize the subtle ways in which white supremacy is expressed. Often Blacks are urged to evaluate everything according to a eurocentric scale. You might remember the old children's ditty recited in the African American community (perhaps in White communities also): "If you're White, you're all right; if you're brown, stick around; if you're Black get back." That little refrain accurately reflects the prevalent political and social environment in America.

Voices for the Future

White supremacy is woven into the fiber of American society with projections of White legends and heroes, such as Tarzan, Davey Crockett, Rocky, and Indiana Jones. These heroes need not be American, they can be James Bond or Crocodile Dundee. Just being a White male is all that is needed to lay claims to all great achievement and exalting all things European.

White supremacy teaches that only European music is "classical"; other highly developed musical forms are called "Jazz" or "Bee Bop." Only European artists are called "the masters"; everything else is "primitive" or "folk art." Only European thought is called "philosophy"; other philosophical thought is referred to as "proverbs" or "sayings." The teachings of white supremacy depict Whites as capable of anything and Blacks as absolutely incompetent. Case in point, one of the most popular radio shows of all time was *Amos and Andy*. The central theme—indeed, the source of its popularity—was the absolute incompetence of virtually every member of the African American community. In the world of *Amos* and *Andy*, there were few if any Whites, there was no oppression, no barriers, there were no obstacles confronting African Americans. Left to their own devices, these African American people were foolish and incompetent. These

Africentricity to the Rescue

themes are repeated today in sitcoms like *Martin* and *The Wayan Bros.*

In today's mass media, African Americans are portrayed as buffoons unencumbered by racism. The function of such a characterization is to establish Blacks as Michelle Holmes says in *Radio Voices* as the "ultimate outsiders", people simply incapable of full and equal participation in American society. African Americans are a group against which all other ethnic groups can feel superior. The relentless teaching of white supremacy has become so normalized in this society that many thought it would never be challenged by any serious mass movement. On a quiz I took in Junior High School I was asked, "Why is Africa known as the dark continent?" The correct answer, I was told, was because little is known of it, an idea that has become institutionalized in American society today.

Michael Rogin, a professor at the University of California at Berkeley and author of *Black Face, White Noise,* said on my NIGHTTALK show, "Anti-Black racism is to America what anti-Semitism was to Eastern Europe. People who are ghettoized today had to be stopped from changing their identities, from passing, integrating, and assimilating were Blacks rather than Jews." Indeed, American racism remains the trump card for many

Whites who are insecure and need people to control. Consider North Carolina's Jesse Helms who, when challenged by Harvey Gant (who is Black), ignored the issues and instead appealed to Whites with ads that implied that the choice really came down to having a Black or White senator represent the state. The vote was decided along racial lines with the White majority voting for Helms. Blacks are continually devalued and Americans are convinced once again that Whites know what is best.

Any effort to challenge the assumptions of white supremacy is frequently dismissed as nothing more than revisionist ranting. But in the final analysis, the truth will not be denied. We must know and understand who we are and where and what we come from. What will we become? What new truth will we establish? What truth about us will future generations hold dear? Africentricity is not just a glorious look back, but a challenge to create a glorious future in the spirit of and in tribute to our ancestors. Africentricity gives honor to God, who has caused us to prevail in the face of evil. We owe it to our Father which art in heaven to be great people. The spirit of truth is upon us, and nothing less than the truth will be accepted.

CHAPTER SIX

From Black Rage to a Blueprint for Change

"We must reinforce argument with results."
Booker T. Washington

In the final decade of the 20th century, the smoldering anger of African Americans is beginning to take shape on various levels. Middle-class Black professionals are finally seeing corporate America's glass ceiling, and many have quit in order to form their own companies.

For the most part, the anger and frustration of Black folks has been expressed primarily on the level of ideas from the fiery rhetoric of Khalid Muhammad to the pointed challenges of Dr. Molefi Asante and others. We have talked about building strong communities, electing progressive young Blacks to office, and calling for national boycotts, but we don't seem to stay angry long enough to effectively set any of these ideas in motion.

The violence—homicides and suicides—coming out of that very same anger is being directed against ourselves. This is not to deny the rare occurrences of a Colin Ferguson, the Black man who walked onto a New York rush hour commuter train and opened fire on innocent suburban commuters. Ferguson said that he was provoked by New York's entrenched racism. In Indianapolis, Mmoja Ajabu, the leader of the Black Panther militia who had been organizing "soldiers," delivered an ultimatum to the city to make government more responsible to Black residents of Indianapolis or face bloodshed. At this point, there has been no bloodshed, violence and anger remain.

Whenever there is a rebellion or riot in the African American community, it has never been the result of some calculated plan of assault seeking revenge on Whites. Often the violence is sparked when a Black youth is killed under suspicious circumstances by a White cop or White mob. In at least one instance, the violence erupted in response to an outrageous miscarriage of jus-tice by an all-White jury. The violence has never occurred because of low performing schools, inadequate health care, or because of the institutional racism that continues to disfigure the lives of far too many African Americans.

There has never been a premeditated use of violence by Blacks against Whites in this country. In fact, the only organized use of violence or acts of terrorism against

Whites has come from other Whites, from lynch mobs and from assassinations that dot the pages of American history. The current right wing militia shootouts, bombing of churches, synagogues, abortion clinics, and the bombing of the Oklahoma federal building are illustrations. Nonetheless, it is the Black community that is most often projected as dangerous and explosive. We are told that Black men are the ones who are naturally prone to violence.

I interviewed Gary Webb author of *Dark Alliance* who examines the CIA and the crack cocaine explosion in this country. The CIA and other government agencies may very well have known of condoned drug trafficking in the Black community. The judicial system consistently fails poor people. The response to this increasing rage bears notice. In Indianapolis, Mayor Stephen Goldsmith is concerned that Black Panther leader Mmoja Ajabu's call to arms may give young Blacks an excuse to wage violence. He concedes that Ajabu's goals are valid and considers him very intelligent.

The continued aggression against Black people feeds the anger. Rather than eliminate oppression, Americans are encouraged to examine how Black people respond to that oppression. Then African Americans are condemned for their incorrect response. When Mayor Goldsmith said that Mmoja Ajabu may incite Blacks to commit violence, he was ignoring the fact that one out of four Blacks in Indianapolis live below the poverty line; the average African American family nationwide earns $17,000 a year *less* than the average White family. The Mayor ignored the litany of unresolved social ills that are the real reasons for the rage that simmers in the Black community.

In the final analysis, African Americans don't need to invent an excuse for violence. The relentless aggression against Blacks is reason enough. In contrast, it is interesting to note, that the Oklahoma bombing of a US federal office building, which killed more than 600 people in the biggest act of terrorism ever on American soil is attributed to "angry white men," not animals or monsters. They're not even characterized as domestic terrorists. However, when Timothy McVeigh was indicted and convicted of this heinous crime, there were those who offered as an excuse the Waco shootout, saying that was the event that drove him to fatalistic despair.

What followed in the wake of the Oklahoma bombing was the nation's attempt to understand what could have provoked this tragic occurrence. At the same time, this very same nation freely dismisses the anger of Blacks as simply irrational. Americans deny that African Americans have any basis for anger. Of course, the denials are set in motion by how Americans discuss race. An America

Online survey conducted during the Spring of 1997 showed that 81 percent of the people surveyed opposed racial and gender preferences in hiring for public jobs and admission to public colleges. However, the question was designed to reassure White males that their renewed racist vigor meets the approval of the American public. The question simply asked, do you favor preferences based on race and sex. To ask about preferences without placing the question in a historical as well as political perspective leaves little choice. Most people felt compelled to vote no.

In the African American community, the debate takes on a very different tone as we ask two significant questions. Should Blacks and women be protected from racism and sexism? Is it still necessary to protect people from racism and sexism? Had AOL asked these questions the survey results would have been dramatically different. But the choice of questions by AOL was not an oversight or mistake on their part. The question was designed to help shape the discussions about race in America toward a conservative perspective. In fact, conservatives attack equal opportunity by using the language of the civil rights movement.

Newt Gingrich and Orrin Hatch say the time has come for all Americans to have equal opportunities in obtaining jobs, contracts, and admissions to universities. They use the language of equal opportunity to make the point that measures taken to repair the damage done by centuries of racism are unnecessary and perhaps illegal. In the Black community it sounds like another attempt to use the law to protect white priviledge!

When President Clinton toyed with the idea of making an apology for slavery, many White Americans did not understand why they needed to apologize; after all, they had not been personally responsible for the enslavement of Africans. Americans are, for the most part, careful to frame discussions in ways that will hide or absolve their guilt. For example, the economy of the old South is often referred to as a plantation economy when, in fact, it was a slave-based economy. The plantation was built on the backs of Africans. As Dr. Claud Anderson makes clear, free Black labor produced white wealth.

For decades, Whites have benefited from a society with special privileges and preferences. Let us be real clear about racism. We are not simply talking about hating your neighbor. Racism is a system in which special advantages are set aside for certain racial groups. During segregation, it was illegal for a Black-owned cab to pick up fares outside the Black Pitts Hills district of Pittsburgh. In other words, the law protected white-owned cabs from fair competition. The larger economic pie was set aside for Whites only. As a result of that kind of social engineering, many businesses that exist to this day owe their start-up and growth to America's racist legacy.

Businesses like the major department store chains boast of their humble beginnings and hard work, but they are in fact the beneficiaries of laws and social policies that set aside bank loans, real estate locations, sales territory, as well as education and training for Whites only. And now, decades after white priviledge, many Whites cannot find one reason to apologize for the consequences of the very system that put their priviledged life-style in motion.

Since special benefits and privileges of Whites remain the most significant obstacles to harmony between the races, any plea for racial harmony must begin with Whites giving up their privilege and sharing all of this nation's resources. Otherwise, the appeal will remain a shallow political ploy. Presently, few Whites are ready to give up their special privileges and play fair. For African Americans the message is clear. Our future is in our own hands. Our challenge is to use our minds, our talent, and all of our resources effectively. We must use them in ways that speak directly to the needs of the African American community. Very often we have responded with what can be called "an emotional response" to our history. Often, I hear the anger nightly from callers around the country. However, we are now at a point in which emotionalism will no longer be sufficient. The future of African Americans will be defined by our carefully developed strategies from past voices and the actions we take.

Shouting or screaming to express anger may be gratifying on an emotional level. It may allow you to vent and release some degree of stress, but shouting and screaming is woefully inadequate on a political and economic level. Remember the old axiom, "success is the best revenge." If we are angry because the D.A. won't indict a White cop or any member of a White mob in the death of an unarmed Black youth, as in the killing of Johnny Gammage in Pittsburgh or the murder of Yusef Hawkins in New York, in addition to marching in protest and calling the local talk shows to vehemently express our outrage, why not identify and vote for a new D.A., one who is committed to the African American community? Stay angry long enough to organize the anger into votes.

Dick Gregory made this point one evening to a small group that included Minister Kevin Muhammed of the Nation of Islam, Rev. Al Sampson from Chicago, Joe Madison, a talk show host from Washington, DC, Rev. Al Sharpton, and myself. We were talking about the CIA crack cocaine connection in South Central Los Angeles. Dick gestured to the New Yorkers in the room and said, "If you guys are really upset in this town, prove it by electing Sharpton Mayor" (Al had recently announced his mayoral candidacy). He had a point. How do we express our anger in a political context? The answer is quite simple. Stay angry long enough to organize something. Turn the anger into energy. Allow the rage to empower your blueprint for meaningful action. And remember, this call for strategic thinking is part of the historical experience of Blacks in America.

Langston Hughes called on the young Black artists of his era to change social conditions through the force of their art. He was referring to how generations of African Americans were encouraged and literally taught to "take low" to protect themselves from a hostile White society. These self-defeating ideas had power because they were subtly passed along for generations by people we loved and trusted. On this eve of a new century, however, it is time to reorganize and uncover the source of the old whispering that, even to this day, suggests that limited goals and extreme caution form the best blueprint for success.

This cautious life-style has historical roots. When I was a teenager hanging out in the community center in the Brooklyn housing project where I grew up, I was, along with many other kids, often counseled by the African American adults who supervised the center. They would urge us to get an education, stay out of trouble, and make our parents proud. Invariably, they would ask, "What do you want to be when you finish school?" When I said I wanted to be an art director in the advertising industry, these well-meaning adults would scold me. They would tell me I should prepare for civil service exams or plan to pursue something more realistic. One of them even snapped, "I wish my son would come home talking about being an art director. I would break his neck." Many African Americans heard this advice from Black and White adults. The best known example is Malcolm X, whose junior high school teacher told him that his dream to become a lawyer was simply impossible and nothing more than faulty thinking and planning on his part. It was Elijah Muhammed whom Malcolm credits for restoring his sense of self-worth.

The "take-low" philosophy survived even as we began to achieve these "unrealistic" goals. It was simply updated to fit the realities of each generation. It went from "you can't do it" to "now that you're here, don't rock the boat." Don't seek or expect recognition and don't be too ambitious. This advice was internalized, because the people who offered it were not enemies (except in the case of Malcolm whose White teacher was trying to break his spirit). For the most part, the people passing along this advice were family, friends, and neighbors, and they were passing along a survival tradition.

From Black Rage to a Blueprint for Change

For many African Americans, the effects of those ideas linger on and are still being passed along. Black politicians say they cannot identify too closely with the African American community as their careers reach new heights. Black professionals avoid political causes, and Black entrepreneurs desire nice little businesses, "nothing too big, just enough to feed my family and pay my bills." Each generation of African Americans is told in one way or another to expect that their success will be less than other racial groups.

We must replace negative thinking with a new perspective. Alice Walker is correct when she says, "No person is your friend who demands your silence or denies your right to grow." We must develop and utilize all of our skills; nothing less is acceptable. In school we are expected to learn reading, math, history, and science; we must continue to learn throughout life. Geoffrey Holder illuminates the need to develop yourself as he has become a dancer, actor, painter, cook, choreographer, and clothing designer.

Consider also the experience of Rhythm and Blues Hall of Famer, Lloyd Price. His career began at age 17 when a local disc jockey invited him to a New Orleans recording studio and asked if he could come up with a good original song. Without hesitation Lloyd replied, "Yes I can." He was then introduced to the piano player who would accompany him on the audition tape, a heavy set youngster named Antoine Domino that everyone called Fats. As Fats began to play, Lloyd began to sing, making it up as he went along. "Lawdy Miss Clawdy" became the first R&B record to sell one million copies. It was the first R&B crossover record and Lloyd's first in a string of 11 million selling gold records.

Lloyd's success began with the words "yes I can." If our thinking becomes strategic, we will create change. We must not allow our outrage, justifiable though it may be, to diminish our creativity. Strategic thinking demands that we focus on clearly defined goals. "It's Nation Time" was a popular phrase during the 1970's. This slogan took on an added dimension when we began to understand that it took skill and resources, as well as emotional stability, to build a nation or community. "It's Nation Time" became a call for African Americans to summon the best of our traditions and talents in order to create a new society. Even when a people are under attack, a new reality or a new society will come as a result of how effectively the people counter the attacks.

W.E.B. DuBois' voice for the future says that "There is in this world no such force that can deter man. The human soul cannot be permanently chained."

CHAPTER SEVEN

Bright Eyed Justice

"And your sin cursed, guilty union shall be shaken to its base, til you learn that simple justice, is the right of every race."
                    Frances Ellen Watkins Harper

The wave of fire bombings of Black churches that have occurred throughout the South since 1990 has forced many Americans to face the uncomfortable truth that anti-Black racism is still very much a part of the nation's political landscape. The response to this ugly reality is a renewed call for racial harmony. There is an effort to resurrect Martin Luther King, Jr.'s call for nonviolence, thus reminding African Americans that one of our unique gifts is the capacity to suffer peacefully. But strangely enough, the calls for peace and harmony have somehow avoided the essential ingredient absolutely necessary for peace, that being *justice*!

Voices for the Future

The violent protests in Los Angeles did not occur simply because a mob of policemen viciously beat Rodney King, nor was it a reaction to the Korean merchant whose bullet in the back of the head killed unarmed African American fourteen-year-old Latasha Hollins. Black people don't expect the government or the White community to control individual behavior. However, the frustration in the African American community was heightened when the judge in the Latasha Hollins case ignored the jury's guilty verdict and refused to sentence the killer! Where was the justice? When the "Rodney King" trial was shifted to Simi Valley, a community populated primarily by police officers and their families, when the jury ignored graphic reality and acquitted a police mob actually caught in the act on videotape, where was the justice? When thousands of people marched to protest the beating and torture of Abner Louima, a Haitian immigrant who alleged that he was tortured at the hands of New York City cops, and the cops are identified but none were charged with any wrong doing, where was the justice?

All of the calls for peace and racial harmony, all of the suggestions for money and government programs are shallow and morally bankrupt and avoid Dr. King's more relevant challenge "To put bright eyed justice back on her rightful throne." Without justice, the recent ap-peal for racial harmony is nothing more than an appeal for business as usual on behalf of arrogant, often racist merchants who thrive in the African American community and who simply want their cash registers to ring without interruption. But for African Americans, the goal must be a fair and just society.

Don't allow the struggle to become entertainment. Don't let it become reduced to who talks the toughest. Don't let the movement for the empowerment of Black people be played out on talk shows. Only intelligent action on a personal and community level will accomplish our goals. "Keep your eyes on the prize" makes sense only if we know and recognize what the prize is. Plainly stated, justice remains the essential ingredient for a peaceful and harmonious society. The scripture explains that without justice there can be no peace. Isaiah's voice for the future says, "And judgment is turned away backward, and justice standeth afar off. For truth is fallen in the street and equity cannot enter" (Isaiah 59:14). In order to establish a society free of racial tension and hostility, in order for the much sought after equity to enter our lives, we need justice to open the door.

At age 82, the esteemed scholar John Hope Franklin has been commissioned by President Clinton to chair the advisory board for the President's race initiative. Dr. Franklin told a group of reporters that he was cautiously optimistic about the future. He said "that while he had a lot of caveats, he had some reservations." African Americans cannot return to business as usual. Our support, politically and economically, must never again be taken for granted. No justice, no peace has to become more than a slogan. It must become a concrete political and economic strategy. Justice is the demand, and it is a fair and just demand. In order to move our drive for justice forward, African Americans must rearrange our political priorities and redirect our energies and our dollars! It is time to begin to do those things that are in our own best interest.

The firebombings of Black churches and violent confrontations between Black men and White policemen, some of which began with a simple traffic violation, often resulted in the death of Black men. We begin to hear faint rumblings of a call for harmony and racial healing, similar to calls made after the infamous Rodney King incident or the 1963 bombing of the 16th Street Baptist Church in Birmingham, Alabama.

Mayor Rudolph Giuliani of New York City wants to avoid racial justice while continuing to set aside the city's resources primarily for Whites. Giuliani's predecessor,

David Dinkins, wanted an administration that reflected the city's "gorgeous mosaic" of diversity, Giuliani has what he calls "one city, one standard." This strategy ignores the city's ethnic makeup and allows him to staff City Hall mostly with Whites. When Blacks complained about the absence of African Americans in the Mayor's inner circles, Giuliani told them they were "excessively fixated" on the notion of ethnic balance that he characterizes as "symbolic government." New York is a city that practically invented balanced ticket politics. Mayor Giuliani is rewriting the rule book. But for Black New Yorkers, the new rules sound very much like the old Jim Crow rules: Whites were entitled to the advantages that came from decades of preferential treatment. Whites know what is best and should govern, and all others will benefit from their wisdom.

The New York press has been extremely supportive of the Mayor. The media promotes that "New York City is a safer, cleaner and wealthier place than it was when Giuliani took over 3 ½ years ago." The media forgets the fact that the city's crime rate began to decline under Mayor David Dinkins and community policing that is credited with making the city safer was instituted by Mayor Dinkin's police commissioner, Lee Brown. A

Harlem resident said the Mayor's removal of street vendors from Harlem's 125th Street has helped make that historic thoroughfare safer. The media ignored the many Harlem residents who have denounced the removal of the vendors who provided employment and a greater diversity of products.

Unemployment continues to climb in the Black community, and small Black vendors and retail merchants on 125th Street have been put out of business to make way for the white-owned megastores like the Gap, Disney, Barnes and Noble, and such. In place of Black economic development, there is, once again, white dominance. Nonetheless, there is much talk about racial harmony.

The pursuit of racial harmony can easily become an empty and hypocritical gesture if the champions of peace and harmony continue to ignore the basic and simple reality of the legacy of justice denied and pretend that all that is needed is a sense of friendship and tolerance. African Americans do not suffer from a lack of White friends or White lovers. We do not suffer from a simple lack of tolerance. While friendship and tolerance are certainly of value, Blacks suffer in this society from a lack of justice. We suffer from decades of policy decisions that have placed the nation's resources disproportionately in the hands of Whites. It is rather convenient to call for racial harmony at a time when imbalance and injustice have been used to institutionalize advantages and special privileges for Whites. These calls for racial harmony are fraudulent if they ignore the challenge to restore fairness and balance to this distorted society.

The real challenge is to revamp court systems, restructure police departments, eliminate bank and real estate red lining policies, eliminate double standards, and simply deal with the litany of racist ills still plaguing America. Somehow, it is easier to erect antiracism billboards with photos of Black and White children playing together than to deal with the real reasons causing the anger and tension. The tragedy is that as the young models in those ads grow up, they will inherit an American society that will allow them to play together but will continue to deny Black children equal access to resources and opportunity.

It has never been an issue of whether or not Whites love Blacks but whether Blacks can expect justice as we pursue our legitimate desires and ambitions. The issue is not one of harmony; the fact that many Blacks and Whites love each other does not prevent churches from burning or Black motorists from being killed by the police. You have heard the refrain "no justice, no peace." Justice is all that is required. Dr. King's voice for the future can still be heard urging us to "Put bright eyed justice back on her rightful throne."

However, Dr. King is not our sole visionary leader. My concern is that 34 years after his "I Have a Dream" speech, too many African American leaders are still urging us to keep the dream alive. Surely after three decades someone else has a newer vision for the future of African Americans. Dr. King's dream of a desegregated society where people are judged solely by the content of their character is still unfulfilled. However, what he fought for in terms of social policy and open accommodations have been accomplished. There is a Black mayor of Atlanta, only a dream in Dr. King's lifetime. Where Bull Connors once terrorized the citizens of Birmingham, Alabama, there is now a talented African American mayor in whom Black and White citizens have placed their confidence. We have seen a Black sheriff in Mississippi, we have seen Blacks employed in industries denied us in Dr. King's lifetime. He would be pleased that much of what he envisioned for America now exists.

But each generation's priorities change as the realities change. I remember Jackie Robinson saying he appreciated all that baseball had done for him, but he was still dismayed by the fact that there were no Black coaches or managers. Today, we have both. As a result, this generation's focus has shifted to the question of ownership. If I can use the baseball field to make the point, old line traditional leadership is still focused on the coaches' box, and we need people who demand ownership.

We are at the point where we must turn our attention to the effective use of the economic and educational resources that we now possess. What does it mean to have world class scholars like Drs. Donald Smith, Asa Hiliard, and Charsee McIntyre and not own academies in which their knowledge can be institutionalized and passed on to benefit future generations? Much of what we accomplish as a people depends on our willingness to stand on our strengths as well as strengthen our resolve to pursue a fair and just society.

Don't be confused by the Black and White defenders of White privilege. There are those who point to the accomplishments of Blacks as an indication that racism is diminishing and that no further action is required to address the inequities of this society. Whenever you choose to fight injustice, be aware that the march to freedom may be a long one. However, there are many victories along the way. There will be African Americans whose talents and skills will defeat racism on various levels. Unfortunately, when a Johnnie Cochran, Reginald Lewis, or a Maya Angelou succeeds, racism is belittled and marginalized. Tyrants find it difficult to admit setbacks or defeat. Many African Americans succeed because of their skill and courage in the face of oppression, not because of the lack of oppression. Don't think that the only Blacks who make it are those who are allowed to make it. Don't let the fact that you will surely encounter opposition scare you. Remember, as George Fraser says, *"Success Runs In Our Race."*

Don't be intimidated by the obstacles or resistance you encounter. In fact, resistance has a way of making us better. It can actually increase your strength. Bodybuilders tell us that the fastest way to build muscle and gain strength is through resistance exercises like weight lifting. In fact, if your muscles don't experience resistance, they begin to shrink and grow weaker. It is when you become complacent that progress ends. Perhaps some middle-class African Americans and some leaders have less reason to fight and confront oppression.

If we accept the illusion of a color blind society, we risk becoming complacent, and white privilege increases.

Black folk need not slow down. In fact, an effective way to overcome obstacles, both personally and collectively, is with bold moves. Dr. Benjamin Mays has cautioned that low aim and self-imposed low expectations are formidable obstacles we place in our own path. It is often bold and audacious action that energizes an individual or a people. Many Black folk who had little faith in electoral politics were fired up by Jesse Jackson's bold bid for the U.S. Presidency in 1984. These enthusiastic voters came out in record numbers on election day. If you want to change your life or political condition, tinkering about the edges is insufficient. Bold, courageous moves not only will fundamentally change your life, they will also serve to thrust you forward.

When I interviewed Reginald Lewis' wife on NIGHTTALK, she said that an important part of Reginald's character was his audacious business behavior. When a deal he went after failed to materialize, he would begin immediately to develop the next deal, and each failure would lead to the pursuit of an even larger venture, until he ultimately triumphed with the purchase of the Beatrice Corporation.

Even though our ultimate goal is to rid America of racism and oppression, let's be clear. As Aseba Tupahache points out, what we are facing is a chronic condition that is rooted in racist domination, a disease that has infected American society and has spread and been normalized ever since the "founding fathers" began to build what they called America on someone else's land. Consider Thomas Jefferson, among others, signing off on a Constitution that would declare "all men are created equal" while he and George Washington, the nation's first President owned slaves. Consider also Whites who, in 1921, became so jealous of the success of their Black neighbors in North Tulsa that they went on a rampage, killing innocent Blacks, burning buildings, and even dropping dynamite from airplanes.

The contradictions continue to this day as random acts of violence are being committed by White mobs, both police and civilians. The September 28, 1997 *New York Times* tells of a Brooklyn community—the scene of a White mob attack on two young Black men—as a community divided by a racial line. Blacks live on one side of the Gowanus Expressway in the section called Red Hook and Whites on the other in Carroll Gardens. The *Times* article quoted a 16-year-old White youth as saying, "It's about boundaries, you pass the line, you get chased out."

Bright Eyed Justice

Whites need to examine their own fears as they attempt to dominate the peoples of the world. Often during the open forum segments on NIGHTTALK, I have asked "What's wrong with White folks?" I believe it is necessary, as we fight against racism, to examine and thereby understand the mindset of Whites. Racism is a deep rooted illness requiring a kind of social surgery to remove it from the very innards of society. Clearly, this is a process that will take generations.

The question for African Americans is clear. Can we continue to move ahead at a prodding pace? Justice is the balm that can provide significant immediate relief for the victims of racism, while the ongoing effort to redeem the soul of America continues.

Regarding the issue of justice, there is another important distinction to be made. We must not confuse justice with revenge. There are those who clamor for death penalties and executions of whomever happens to be in custody. The prosecutors in Philadelphia chose to ignore glaring evidence that Mumia Abu-Jamal was denied a fair trial. This evidence has been accepted by jurists and citizens throughout the world. Still the judge in that case, Judge Sabo, ignores the evidence and suggests that revenge for the death of the policeman Mumia is accused of shooting is all that is required, a fair trial is not.

Voices for the Future

A Midwestern couple camps outside of penitentiaries whenever an execution is scheduled, to show support for the execution. They have been doing this ever since the execution of someone convicted of killing a member of their family. They are gratified by the death of other people and any life will do. Revenge has replaced justice.

There are those who still refuse to hear Isaiah's voice as he says, "none calleth for justice, nor any pleadeth for truth, they trust in vanity and speak lies. They conceive mischief and bring forth inequity" (Isaiah 59:4). African Americans must not be confused. What we want is a fair and just society. Vengeance is in God's hand. His challenge to us is clear. "Defend the poor and fatherless. Do justice to the afflicted and needy." (Psalms 82:3)

CHAPTER EIGHT

An Open Letter to Black Music Radio and the Music Industry

"Let the music take your mind"
Sly Stone

The critical issue facing the African American community is not simply crime and violence. The more profound challenge is on the level of values. The kids on the street are miseducated and misguided; their violence and arrogance reflect a distorted value system that is unaware of the principles and traditions that have held African American communities together in spite of oppression.

Black music radio has the ear of this generation, like it or not, accept it or not. You are their primary source of information. And while some may argue that it is the parents' responsibility to introduce and instill values, let me remind you of the saying of our ancestors, "It takes a whole village to raise the children." You, my brothers and sisters, are a part of the village. These are your children also. Since you have their ear, you have a unique opportunity to introduce life giving values and ideas.

At this critical time, when violence and confusion abound, the more music, less talk approach does our community a disservice. There are intelligent radio personalities on your stations who are caring parents themselves. Allow them to do more than time, weather, and call letters. Let them help us reclaim the minds of our young.

While everyone clamors for more police, more prisons, and stiffer penalties, some of us must talk to the hearts and minds of a generation whose lives are being destroyed on the streets where they live. Help us instill a family-and-community-centered value system. There is time between records to challenge and inspire African American youth to respect themselves, and difficult though it may be, choose a better way to carve out a future for themselves and their families.

The death of Tupac Shakur and Biggie Smalls caused the music moguls to pause for only a moment, just

An Open Letter to Black Music Radio and the Music Industry

long enough to bury the dead and return to their dangerous enterprise where violence, pimps (romantically called players), and 1930's style "gangstas" are offered to African American youth. The tragic fact is that in this society, criminal enterprise is the only truly profitable "work" available to large numbers of young African Americans—unless they are encouraged to resist the contradictions in this society rather than seek only a piece of the action.

An article published by the *San Jose Mercury News* confirms what many of us have always suspected: The government helped spread the sale of crack cocaine among L.A.'s African American street gangs. Our young people are being conned into an illusionary world of false power and meaningless prestige. A world without a future. Radio personality, Imhotep Gary Byrd, reminds us that it is a question of choices when he says, "The key to tomorrow is what you choose today, the decision to work or whether to play. Both have their place in the human life stream, but only one will achieve your dream."

But our young cannot choose life if death is all they are taught. They cannot choose love if lust is all you exalt. They cannot choose God if Satanism is all you feed them. Since you already have their attention and access to their minds, I urge the Black decision makers in the radio and music industry to consider well the very seeds you plant in the minds of our youth. At some point you may very well have to answer for it.

This is by no means the first attempt to urge the Black music industry to be more responsive to the needs of the community. People like Oscar Brown, Jr., Stevie Wonder, Gil Scott Heron, Curtis Mayfield, Sweet Honey and the Rock, Kenny Gamble, and Leon Huff have always understood the power of the music and have found ways to make the music serve the people.

We love our music, even though African American literature has historically been our primary liberating force. The masses of our people were not reading Martin Delany, Frederick Douglass, Richard Wright, Langston Hughes, James Baldwin, John Killens, Amiri Baraka, Ishmel Reid, Sonia Sanchez, and other liberating writers.

For the masses it was always the music. Music is the literature of the people. As eloquently as the authors wrote "Black is Beautiful," it wasn't until James Brown sang "Say it loud. I'm Black and I'm proud" that the masses really heard it. The music was always operating at the center of the forces moving and shaping the African American community. It not only reflected the dismal reality, but in the hands of gifted singers, it became Malcom and Garvey set to a beat. The message from the picket lines and the street corners was being reinforced on concert stages and on the radio. Could the current violence against women exist unabated with Otis Redding explaining the value of "Trying A Little Tenderness" while Aretha explained that "a woman's not a plaything? She's flesh and blood like her man."

Given the continual effort to dehumanize African Americans, we need to hear Curtis Mayfield tell us that "You're a winner." We need to hear Stevie encourage us to "Keep on reaching for higher ground." Could the negative attitudes toward African American women exist in the music climate set by Smokey Robinson, Marvin Gaye, the Four Tops, the Temps, and all the love men from Jerry Butler to Jon Lucien?

Could it be so easy to disrespect African American women when the images you saw were Gladys Knight, Dionne Warwick, and Kim Weston? Righteous sisters who keep their clothes on and simply sang like angels. For the masses, this was the Black arts renaissance, music and ideas and a life giving energy that came from the culture of African people. It was, in fact, a cultural expression that helped to clarify our consciousness and create emotional attitudes which were conducive to action.

And this is why the message was suppressed and exchanged for a music without vision. A new energy was introduced into the African American community. Despair and lust are celebrated as reality, and the radio disc jockey, who was once smooth and articulate, who kept the community informed, was replaced by more music and a less talk format. The White consultants who removed talk and personality from Black radio simply did not understand the emotional value of a Hank Spann of WWRL radio in New York periodically reminding his audience, that "before we can get up, you got to get down." Everyone in the African American community understands that "get down" means to get serious, and whatever you

An Open Letter to Black Music Radio and the Music Industry

are doing, do it well.

What is needed is a rebirth of the cultural arts movement—music, literature, images, and film totally committed to the empowerment of the African American community. We must return to the level of liberating ideas. Artists and political activists must be on the same mission; they must resist the seductions of a weaker moral self while moving to sustain a stronger spiritual and more perfect self. The true role of the artist and activist must go beyond protest to become shapers of the future reality. The Black artist must link his work to the struggle for the liberation of his people. Unfortunately, the best efforts of Black artists seem trapped within a music industry that has always been willing to sacrifice the interest of the artist and community in order to control the profits and the flow of ideas.

Oscar Brown, Jr. once told me that we will have to free the music so that the awesome power of the music can free the people. A conscious Black arts movement is what is needed. I have a reasonable request for African

Voices for the Future

American music industry executives: Just as you have found innovative ways to serve your bosses, perhaps you can find some small way to serve your people.

CHAPTER NINE

Hip vs. Smart

> *We are beautiful, but there is more work to do. And just being beautiful is not enough, therefore, what we are asking for is a new synthesis, a new sense of reality....*
>
> Larry Neal

We have a simple choice—either submit to oppression or fight our oppressors. Many Blacks have chosen to respond to racist aggression by perfecting a sense of style that gives the appearance of freedom and power. In the process, activism is rejected. In fact, activists are characterized as the source of the community's problems in that they protest entirely too much against racist acts. They explain their own lack of activism with statements like "everybody is active in their own way" or "I don't join groups."

For some, it is quite important to eat in the trendiest restaurants, wear designer clothing, drive the right car

(BMWs in the 1980's, Range Rovers in the 1990's) and hang out at the appropriate night spots, ski clubs, and golf courses (in the 1970's, it was the tennis courts). Black organizations must book their annual conferences at the most expensive hotel or resort, preferably with a casino.

I am not denouncing or denigrating these pursuits, but many of us have substituted the material symbols of success for true achievement and real power. We're working, but what we're actually achieving is the illusion of power and success.

The challenge for African Americans is the setting of new priorities based on a newer sense of social reality. To begin with, let's learn to distinguish between hip and smart. Blacks, and particularly our youth, are encouraged, if not manipulated, to embrace "hip" as an appropriate life-style. Hip people shop in the most fashionable stores, but—smart people own the stores. Hip people dine at the trendiest restaurants, smart people own the restaurants. It's hip to drive the right car, it's smart to own the dealership. Hip people have nicknames such as Daddy Cool, Mack Daddy, Money, Slick, and the like, while smart people have titles such as chairman, president, and CEO.

The voices for the future are challenging us to make

smart choices instead of hip ones. The quality of life for African Americans will depend on our willingness to move from the comfortable tradition of hip choices to the more progressive level of smart choices. Hip culture is individualistic.

For most of our existence, Black people have settled on making hip choices. We have chosen ways to express our desire for power and prestige in the way we dress and in the stylish cars we drive. We have a certain flair for living with grace and style in the midst of despair. It is undoubtedly the grace and style that make these substitutes for real power so gratifying.

African Americans turned work songs and the wails of a suffering people into sensuous blues lyrics that spoke to issues of love and redemption. In the face of great despair, Black folk sang. So sweet were our songs they delighted the oppressor. The Hebrews of the old testament lamented that "for them that carried us away captive required of us a song. They that wasted us required of us mirth, saying sing us one of the songs of Zion" (Psalms 137:3). In the midst of despair, Black folks found comfort in our ability to put a little glide in our stride, a little cut in our strut. It's our unique sense of style that distinguishes our presence in America. Finally, we must understand that style, hip though it may be, is not enough.

Part of our legacy, is our ability to take a little and make it last. From tattered fabrics, we made glorious patchwork quilts. From a shaft of corn, we made corn bread, corn pudding, corn on the cob, corn kernels, and so on. We turned discarded parts of a pig into soul food delicacies.

Looking back at their childhood, many Black Americans recount how they were poor and didn't know it. The way Black folk carved a way out of no way did indeed sustain us. On one level, a hip style became the expression of our humanity. The problem occurred when we learned to substitute style for substance.

Racism cannot prevent some Blacks from rising and succeeding. Its intention is to prevent Blacks as a group from achieving power and influence. In fact, the success of a few individuals is not only tolerated but actually encouraged. These individuals who are not the least threatening to Whites create the illusion of progress sufficient to satisfy the entire group. I wonder how many African Americans have been pacified because of the success of Michael Jordan, Bill Cosby, Oprah Winfrey, Michael Jackson, and a few others. The presence of a few Black millionaires has no effect on the miseducation of our children and the police brutality of our people.

Whatever becomes of us either on a personal or group level is the result of the choices we make. Our condition today is due to the choices we made yesterday. Tomorrow will be shaped and developed by the choices we make today. People are constantly making choices, but many of them are made subconsciously from our "second nature." To improve your condition, however, your choices, and thus your behavior, must become more conscious. We must carefully consider the consequences of our actions. African Americans, like many other people, usually react to their social and political environment. Deepak Chopra says, "We are conditioned through repetition to respond to stimuli in certain predictable ways." To become better decision makers, we must become conscious and proactive.

When Whites refuse to have a Black doctor, accountant, or attorney, they are making a choice that reinforces the illusions of white supremacy, not to mention keeping their dollars in the White community. We often choose professionals of different races to demonstrate that we are free of any bias. The long-term consequence of this choice is that our own competent professionals are not being supported. More importantly, when Blacks choose to ignore the talents and services of other African Americans, they also reinforce the illusion of white supremacy. They are reacting according to a response that was created centuries ago. We don't set out to harm our own, but that is the effect of the unconscious choices we make.

We live in a free country, you may argue. We have freedom and the right to choose. We are free to wear expensive clothes, even if we never purchase anything from a Black owned-business, free to vacation anywhere, eat anywhere, party anywhere, even deposit millions of dollars in white banks that do not make loans to African Americans. It is important to understand the consequences of the choices we make on a daily basis.

When you consider the life-style affected by many Blacks, it cannot be denied that we are hip. In order to become a new people, however, radical change will be necessary. Old habits will have to be discarded. The future is indeed shaped by the choices we make on a daily basis. Everything we do has an impact on the overall quality of our lives. All of our actions are related and nothing exists in a vacuum. We understand that our behavior strengthens or weakens the Black community. In that sense, where you shop, bank, or dine is a political choice. What you read, what you eat, how and where you spend your time helps to develop who you are. Scripture refers to the importance of choices when it says you will reap what you sow. So consider carefully the outcomes of each and every decision you make. Will your family benefit? Will your people benefit? If not, then you should reconsider your decisions. We must change individually to create change as a group.

In a recent NIGHTTALK interview with Dr. Frances Cress Welsing, we talked about the importance of smart decision making. Dr. Welsing said that raising children in the midst of a hostile white society is a very serious undertaking for Black parents. To have children and to maximize their growth and development is to take on a great responsibility. Having children is not child's play. Thus, Dr. Welsing advises that African Americans should choose to have children when the mother is 30 years old and the father is at least 35. This would be decision making based on a realistic understanding of American social conditions. Deepak Chopra, in his book *The Seven Spiritual Laws of Success*, says, "The more you make choices on a conscious level, the greater your chances of engaging in correct behavior."

As we approach the new millennium, something new is required of African Americans. When we consider the sum total of our talents, training, and our intellectual capital, as well as our financial capital; when you consider that God has never abandoned us, here at the dawn of a new century, certainly style must now give way to substance. We must use the best of our traditions and experiences as a blueprint for creating a new community and in real sense a new people. The challenge is clear, we must move from hip to smart. That would be really hip!

CHAPTER TEN

Respect Yourself

RESPECT/re'spek/n 1: an act of giving particular attention: consideration 2a: high or special regard: esteem b: the quality or state of being esteemed expression of respect or deference 3: to consider worthy of high regard.

To respect yourself is to honor and cherish yourself, to hold yourself in high esteem.

Youngsters in my Respect Yourself summer softball league are taught that they can accomplish any goal, that they can turn any dream into a reality because their lives are an expression and example of God's genius. As God's creations, they are living miracles. Life itself is a miracle. You exist through no calling of your own. Life is God's wonderful, miraculous gift.

How we live our lives is what causes us to lose sight of our divine nature. Without that awareness of who we really are, without that connection to our spiritual self, without the link to the presence of God within, as Susan Taylor says, "Ours becomes a halting, feeble existence because we are living without the benefit of our greatest strength."

As you begin to understand the divine nature of your life, you are compelled to hold yourself in high regard. You understand that each day of your life is another day that the miracle continues. You must constantly explore how great you can become and learn to avoid anything that can destroy your potential.

We must understand respect as it applies to daily life. All that you may achieve and all that you become can be directly linked to how you feel about yourself. It has been said that people do not attract what they want but who they are. What we become is shaped by how we feed and nourish our very being, and how you treat yourself depends on how you feel about yourself.

When someone owns a fine and expensive car, they usually take excellent care of it. They give the automobile regular tune ups, premium gasoline, and fine grades of oil. Often, they won't allow eating in the car, and by no means are younger siblings allowed to borrow the automobile. Same thing with people who own expensive, high quality audio equipment, or computers. They also

Respect Yourself

tend to protect the components and avoid harsh use. They value their equipment, and the more expensive it is, the greater care the items are given.

Many of these same people who hold fine automobiles and audio equipment in high esteem seem to forget the meaning of value and high regard when it comes to the care of their own mind and bodies. They put harmful substances in their bodies; too many sweets, too much salt, alcohol, junk food, nicotine, and in some instances, drugs. They would never subject their fine automobiles to such abuse, yet they treat themselves this way. When you truly respect something, you carefully nourish and protect it. When you truly respect yourself, you begin to see your mind and body as worthy of great care.

The Black community remains the one community in which cigarette smoking and alcohol use has not declined. It is helpful to understand that what you eat and drink not only affects your health but also reflects the extent to which you respect yourself. When you truly consider yourself to be of great value, you will guard against those things that are harmful to you. When you further consider that 90 percent of the diseases prevalent in the African American community could be prevented by avoiding harmful food and drink, the decision to continue to destroy our health with too much salt, scotch, pork, and the like reflects a subtle, if not subconscious, level of disregard for our own being. In the final analysis, it is necessary to examine our lives through a wholistic lens that examines all of our thoughts, decisions, emotions, and behaviors and the consequences of those behaviors on the quality of our lives.

How and where you spend your leisure time, what you read, listen to, and look at (movies, radio, and TV) is largely determined by what you think of yourself. You should only entertain ideas, activities, and people you think are worthy of you. When you hold yourself in high-esteem, you don't accept fear or doubt because it's not worthy of you. There's a gospel song that says, "Lord lift us up where we belong." Up is our destiny. Don't accept being down because it's not worthy of you.

Respect is more than good manners; it is appropriate behavior on every level. When you truly respect yourself, you are careful of who you let in your home, in your heart, and in your bed. When you respect yourself, you are very careful about your sexual relationships. Recognizing that you are your own most valuable resource and that what becomes of you depends on you, it logically follows that you must cherish and protect yourself.

Respect Yourself

Without a doubt, adversity will confront you. Your challenge lies in how you handle it, and that depends on your consciousness, or more so, what you believe about yourself.

Some people accept defeat and setbacks as though failure is inevitable. Others expect to fail, so they are pleasantly surprised when they accomplish a goal. There are also those who fully expect to succeed no matter the task. What separates one from the other is how each person has groomed and nurtured his or her own heart and mind. As you are your own most valuable resource, it is important that growth and development be an ongoing process throughout life. You have the power to shape your own future. We know that this society does not offer African Americans a level playing field or, as Langston Hughes noted, "life for me ain't been no crystal stair." But even in the midst of a repressive social reality, you have the power to change your circumstances by changing your thoughts.

Being in talk radio has given me the opportunity to be in touch with and interview many winners and achievers. From superstar entertainers like Stevie Wonder and Ray Charles whose challenges are obvious, to authors like Iyanla Vanzant, to politicians and entrepreneurs like Wally

(Famous) Amos whose challenges were different, though no less difficult. While these super achievers had in common a strong work ethic and an intense desire to succeed, I noticed something more in their characters that distinguished them from other people. They were confident, assured, and believed they were of value. They respected themselves and demanded it from others.

In the hearts and minds of achievers is a belief that they were born to win. In his book *As A Man Thinketh,* James Allen explains, "As a being of power, intelligence, and love, and the lord of his own thoughts, man holds the key to every situation and contains within himself that transforming and regenerative agency by which he may make of himself what he wills." Achievers always see themselves as the masters of their own fate. Even in their weakest or lowest moments they still cherish themselves as beings of great value with the power to shape their own destiny. Their power rests in what they believe about themselves. The key to transforming your life and setting a course of achievement and success is in fully understanding what it means to believe in yourself, to hold yourself in high esteem, to truly cherish yourself, to understand in the most profound sense that this is what it means to respect yourself.

Respect Yourself

Dempsey Travis is a successful Chicago real estate developer who launched his quest for success on Chicago's South Side in the 1930's where racism was inescapable. In his book *I Refuse to Fail,* Travis explains that the seeds for success in the face of adversity, including racism, were planted in him at the tender age of five by his mother. Travis' family had the distinction of being the first African Americans to live in an apartment building on Cottage Grove Avenue, on Chicago's South Side. Young Dempsey was often taunted with racial insults by a group of White children who also lived there.

Dempsey recalls how his mother, using a black velvet jacket to make her point, made him understand his intrinsic value. She explained that the jacket was beautiful, of high quality, very expensive, and of great value, and that even if ignorant people did not appreciate it, the jacket did not change. It remained a thing of great value and beauty regardless of their ignorance. His mother told him that he was like that jacket, and no matter what anyone else said, he was indeed very precious to her. This simple exchange taught Dempsey "the wisdom of relating to my Blackness in a very positive way."

Travis' parents taught him that internalizing negative and grossly inaccurate self-images about our Blackness ensures failure. They gave him a flight plan for success, one that eventually lifted him above the economic and psychological pitfalls that trap many African Americans and effectively limit our aspirations. Essentially, they taught him to respect himself. This respect was not dependent on the opinions or approval of others. This respect was about a personal sense of value. Self-respect lifted Dempsey above the traps of the historic double consciousness that W.E.B. DuBois talks about in *Souls of Black Folk,* in which he explains that American society imposes a heavy toll on the psyche of the African American. In a world which yields him no true self-consciousness, Dr. DuBois says that "It is a peculiar sensation, this double consciousness, this sense of always looking at one's self through the eyes of others, of measuring one's soul by the tape of a world that looks on in amused contempt and pity."

Recreating ourselves poses a formidable challenge under the best of circumstances. Recreating the African self in the midst of a racist society is even more difficult, yet it can be done. In his classic work *The Mis-Education of the Negro,* Dr. Carter G. Woodson says, "Western education has consistently conformed to the program of the usual propaganda to engender in whites a race hate for Negroes, and in the Negroes contempt for themselves." Respecting ourselves and recreating ourselves anew requires us to change and develop a new perspective.

As the Samurai say, "We must become new." Japanese behavior and psychology are best understood in the ancient strategies of the martial arts. If you start feeling snarled up and you're making no progress, toss your mood away and think in your heart that you are starting everything anew. The Samurai felt that it was essential to understand "becoming new," and so it is with African Americans. A new self is necessary to destroy the consequences of oppression still echoing in our minds.

For many generations, African Americans were taught strategies for success that were designed to escape the attention of a hostile White society. Slaves developed a communications code through song and symbolic sermons that the plantation owner could not fully comprehend. Many generations of African Americans were cautioned to avoid attracting attention. We were taught to "take low." Don't appear too prosperous and don't be too ambitious. The term "Negro rich" meant an acceptable amount of wealth that would not exceed or anger Whites.

As a result, there is a lingering belief that in order to succeed, African Americans must first set "realistic goals." Realistic in this sense means limited. Benjamin Mays' voice for the future told students, "reach for the moon, because even if you miss the moon, you will fall among the stars." It is not just the obstacles that hinder us, but our own low aim.

As we begin to respect ourselves, our behavior begins to change. When you respect your mind you will, of course, avoid thinking self-defeating negative ideas. You will even reject harmful people. However, it is important to keep in mind that rejecting the bad is only step one to becoming a new, more powerful and more prosperous person.

You must feed you mind and spirit even as you feed your body. Your mind has wings. How high you fly in life, how far you go, depends, of course, on the strength of your wings. In other words, the success of your personal flight plan depends not only on your level of consciousness, but on the sharpness of your mind. Therefore, it is important to read, study, and engage in activities that will develop the wings of your mind.

Respect Yourself

Carter G. Woodson reminded us in 1930 to plan with the future in mind. As African Americans face the future, it will be necessary to use our intellectual capital and gifts effectively. These gifts will be of little value if we do not discover and fully develop them. Often we are hindered by distractions that literally "block the blessing." These distractions include destructive habits like drinking until drunk, doing drugs, wasting time in bars, or glued in front of TV sets allowing damaging concepts and dangerous levels of misinformation to enter your mind. We must clear a path to our talents and inner strengths and eliminate negative traits that clutter our lives and often prevent us from maximizing our potential.

Part of the difficulty in moving beyond what are clearly self-defeating habits is that even though they may be negative, these habits become comfortable. We all know people who spend hours in front of mindless, even insulting TV sitcoms and tabloid talk shows. Many will even admit the possibility that what they are doing is harmful.

How often have you heard someone, or even yourself, say, "I know I should not eat this," then devour it anyway? The real challenge to neutralizing habits and clearing a path to the powers within will be in overcoming. It is the power of self-respect that demands that we move beyond our comfort zone to the creating of new behavior.

As you begin to chart a new course for your life, something inside seems to resist. You want to stay the way you have always been. The whispering inner voice asks, "Who do you think you are?" and "What makes you think you can achieve these new goals?" The way to overcome resistance and silence all the voices of despair, the whispering ones inside your head and the loud ones in the world, is to internalize the concept of greater respect for yourself.

When your self-esteem declines, resistance to change gains strength. When you don't believe that you're entitled to succeed, you'll accept less than your best. When you truly hold yourself in high regard, you commit to enhancing your life on every level. Because you respect yourself, you insist on the best for yourself, and every day you work on renewing your mind. As Aretha Franklin reminds us, "All I want is a little R-E-S-P-E-C-T!"

CHAPTER ELEVEN

Therefore

"Do not be satisfied with secondhand or thirdhand things in life. Do not be satisfied until you have put yourselves into that atmosphere where you can seize and hold on to the very highest and most beautiful things that can be got out of life."

Booker T. Washington

On NIGHTTALK, we talk a lot about the inappropriate behaviors displayed by Blacks. African American progress is hindered by the tension between Black men and women, the collapse of the Black family, and the assault on the Black community by White supremacists. My callers clearly understand the history of the oppression of Africans worldwide.

We know that we have been conspired against, socially engineered, exploited, and manipulated. African

Americans have been the target of a relentless racist assault for centuries, an assault that set out to subjugate Africans psychologically as well as physically. The plan was to steal Africans from their land, turn them into sub humans (the U.S. Constitution defined African slaves as 3/5 of a human being), reinvent Africans as Negroes, then steal Africa from the hearts and minds of these so-called Negroes.

The oppression of Blacks, while often denied by Whites, has been well documented and scrutinized by historians, scholars, and activists. The "Negro dilemma," as it has been called, has always been clearly articulated. Consider this letter written to Thomas Jefferson from Benjamin Banneker in 1792. Jefferson was, at the time, Secretary of State. In that letter, Banneker speaks with pride in referring to his own sense of identity when he says, "Sir, I freely and cheerfully acknowledge that I am of the African race and in that color which is natural to them of the deepest dye." There was no attempt here to abandon his Blackness or his brethren.

Clearly, African American people have always been aware of their political and social circumstances. However, during these latter days of the 20th century, it seems that we are still suffering from what Dr. King called the "paralysis of analysis." The key to the next level of achievement for African Americans could be in the strategic use of one word: *therefore*. This might be the most important word in the vocabulary of Black folks at this juncture in our history. This word can be used on both a personal level and group level. After everything is said, after all the facts and angles have been considered, the word "therefore" becomes the catalyst for action. It is the question that moves us to act on what we have been talking about.

For instance, when the facts make it clear that public schools are failing to teach the children or that a mayor is insensitive or that the popular soul food diet is harmful to the health of Black people, after all has been said, insert the word "*therefore.*" The Mayor is insensitive, *therefore*...; the schools don't teach, *therefore*.... *Therefore* compels you to develop a solution, or to at least realize that you don't have one. *Therefore* connects the analysis—the first part of the sentence—to the solution—the second part.

Voices for the Future

This much is clear: There has been insufficient improvement in the psychological, economic, and political status of African Americans in the last few decades—*therefore* fundamental changes are necessary in terms of our overall strategy to empower the Black community. What is necessary is a new willingness to discover the potential within the community, to use the vast intellectual, as well as financial, capital of the Black community to adopt a strategy that will allow Blacks to use our own resources to achieve the necessary level of self-sufficiency.

The move to this level is long overdue when you consider the history of African Americans. Sojourner Truth, Paul Cuffe, Absalom Jones, Richard Allen, and Martin Delany were among the first to raise the issue of self-sufficiency for African people. The Philadelphia Free African Society laid the foundation for the first major Black-owned businesses, the Negro Insurance Companies of the Jim Crow era. President Richard Allen, also founded Allen A.M.E. Church, a major Black religious institution to this day.

Using a slogan he borrowed from Delany, "Africa for Africans," Marcus Garvey built the impressive United

Therefore

Negro Improvement Association during the 1920's. Carlos Cooks founded the African Nationalist Pioneer Movement. The largest mass movement among African Americans organized around "do for self" is, of course, the Nation of Islam, founded by Elijah Muhammed.

Necessary though it may be, this move toward nationalism has often frightened Blacks as well as Whites. Whites sense a loss of control and dominance. Blacks fear that their independence will separate them from Whites and, *therefore*, separate them from the American mainstream. Malcolm's voice for the future says, "Black Nationalism only means that the Black man should control the political economy in his own community." In fact, it is only when African Americans develop and effectively use their own power that they will be able to enter into meaningful alliances with other groups as equal partners.

Now that our history and our present conditions have been placed into perspective, we are compelled to ask, *therefore*...? In short, what do we propose to do about it? Consider the following: The economy in the Black community is failing. African Americans are becoming permanent members of the underclass.

Therefore

Radical changes must occur psychologically and economically. Blacks will have to understand that the American system was never designed for Blacks to share the economic pie. Like other groups, Blacks will have to create a pie of their own, an attractive option in this new global economy.

Dr. Claud Anderson offers PowerNomics, a plan that calls on Blacks to create and control specific industries where Black dollars are significant. Case in point: The Black hair care industry. Only Black people buy Black hair care products. The American Health and Beauty Aids Association says that most supermarkets in white areas won't carry products with African American models on the package because Whites will not purchase them. White housewives don't even buy diapers in packages with Black babies on the front of the package. There are many items that are only being purchased by Blacks, yet there is little involvement by Blacks on the level of ownership. These White owners do not advertise in Black media nor contribute to local causes. As Malcolm X said, "They take our money to the other side of town when the sun goes down."

Therefore

Black entrepreneurs should manufacture more hair care products, own some of the distribution companies, own the local beauty supply stores in the African American community, and publish some of the hair style magazines. Rather than try to convince others to rebuild the Black community, Blacks will have to assume that responsibility ourselves. Rather than adopting a strategy that limits our aspirations to seeking jobs, African Americans must create their own jobs by building industries, as well as assuming more control over the industries we patronize. In addition to Black hair care, African Americans should control the production and distribution of their literature and music.

Ownership is universally recognized as the key to economic viability. Stop gap programs being offered in Black communities such as the Model Cities programs of the 1960's, the enterprise zones of the 1970's, and the empowerment zones of the 1990's are of limited value to the residents of those communities since they provide, for the most part, menial jobs, not careers. Ownership and wealth generated by new construction and the creation of new business remains in the hands of already well established white corporations.

The new economic paradigm shift in the Black community calls on Blacks to think in terms of owning key industries. Another part of the strategy calls on national Black organizations to enter into covenants with Black-owned businesses in the same manner that they have done with white businesses.

In order to change the behavior of corporate America and help to eliminate their racist policies, organizations like the Urban League, NAACP, and Rev Jesse Jackson's PUSH (People United To Save Humanity) have entered into agreements with corporations like Pepsico, Revlon, Denny's, and most recently Texaco. According to these agreements, if the corporation will hire and promote more Black employees, spend more advertising dollars in Black-owned media, deposit some of the money earned in African American markets into Black banks, and do business with Black vendors, then the major civil rights organizations will do their part to increase African American consumption, thus driving billions of Black consumer dollars into the coffers of corporate America. In effect, covenants are marketing plans that declare that Black consumers will be persuaded to spend with white corporations. Although a few African American companies will benefit with new business, the end result is that these Black companies will serve the goal of the marketing plan: *Increase Black dollars in white companies.*

The latest covenant with Texaco suggests that African Americans are still receiving less for their money. One year after the NAACP/Texaco agreement, of Texaco's top executives, 330 were white and only 9 were Black, up from 7 the previous year. Black spending has reached almost $500 billion, yet Black businesses continue to fail. It is clear that a new thrust on the part of African Americans is quite necessary. Since 1994, four premiere Black advertising agencies have gone out of business, and six remain according to the November 1997 issue of *Crain's New York Business*. Times are particularly difficult for Black advertising agencies, even though hip hop urban trends are big business. Undoubtedly, it is time for African Americans to agree to expand our support for each other.

Let's consider another critical issue facing African Americans. Low performing schools are failing African American children at a disproportionate rate at all grade levels.

Voices for the Future

Therefore

Blacks must create an alternative to the public schools. We must create an independent school system to educate our children. It is often argued that the poor performance of African American students is a result of their environment. The argument continues that if family and community provide a nurturing environment conducive for learning and achieving, then and only then will children do well in school. This view tends to ignore the potential of the environment in the school to equip the student to overcome the environment outside the schools.

In a NIGHTTALK interview with world class educator George McKenna, former Compton, California superintendent credited with a miraculous turnaround of that district, he made the point that the unique value of schooling is the school's capacity to educate in spite of the student's social condition. In fact it is an education that empowers students to improve their social condition.

There are many examples of school success. New York's Boys and Girls High School under the leadership of Frank Mickens or Detroit's Malcolm X Academy, where Dr. Clifford Watson is principal. However, the most successful schools are independent, like the Cush campus school in Brooklyn, New York and the W.E.B. DuBois Learning Academy in Kansas City. Their success can be linked directly to the commitment of staff and careful attention to curriculum and instruction.

Dr. Israel Fribble, Jr., President of the Florida Endowment Fund for Higher Education, has said, "The mission of the public schools is to preserve and transmit the majority culture." They therefore, will never by themselves, become revolutionary agents of change. The only change that is likely to occur within the school context is change which does not potentially threaten the status quo of the majority group. Once we recognize that schools will never embrace radical change, we can then explore another route: establishing settings outside of the schools for solutions to the historical patterns of Black children failing academically and socially.

Two excellent ethnic examples are the Jewish-American and Asian-American communities. They both have successfully created supplemental learning environments that run parallel to the mainstream school experience and nurture within children the necessary drive for academic achievement.

Just as other groups have done, African Americans will have to construct a meaningful independent alternative to the public schools; at the same time, the children trapped in public schools throughout the nation cannot be abandoned. The struggle to improve public schools must be intensified. Ultimately, however, the future of succeeding generations of Blacks must be firmly in the hands of Blacks. The minds of Black students cannot be entrusted to people who hold them in contempt.

There are many areas of concern that can be addressed by African Americans using the word *Therefore* as a change agent. In many Black communities, the political leadership does not serve those communities well. *Therefore?....* The Black church does not provide the full leadership it is capable of, *therefore....* There remains a self-defeating tension between Black men and Black women, *therefore?...*

I will not attempt to offer answers to all the challenges facing the African American community in this discussion, since many of the voices have already been provided by so many, from Richard Allen to Reverend Johnny Ray Youngblood and Reverend Calvin O. Butts. From

Therefore

Mary McLeod Bethune to Adelaide Sanford, from Phyllis Wheatley to Sonia Sanchez, from Frederick Douglass to Malcolm X, the blueprint is now, and has for some time, been right here among us.

The word "*therefore*" will force us to the next level—the level of implementation. Clearly, it is time to get busy acting on what we already know we must do.

Therefore, for me, perhaps the most important issue is the question of the Spirit. The spiritual infrastructure of the African American community is suffering. Part of the reason for the continued turmoil in the African American community is our failure to let the power of God intervene on our behalf. When I joined an antiviolence march in what is called the East New York section of Brooklyn, the local ministers leading the march had the marchers hold hands for prayer before stepping off to walk through the community. For these ministers, the prayer was more than a symbolic gesture. It was an effort to infuse our initiative with the extraordinary power of the spirit of righteousness, a power that we believe is here for us even now.

There has been much talk lately of the value of the

power within. Many have agreed that there is a higher power that controls the universe and all therein. This is the same higher power that also lives within each individual, whether we accept it or not. Often, like the beggar at the temple door, we either fail to recognize or underestimate the depth of that holy power. The scripture tells of a beggar, a certain man, lame from birth, who was laid daily at the gate of the temple which was called Beautiful so that he could beg for alms from those entering the temple. One day as he sat at the gate, the Apostles Peter and John approached him to enter the temple. He stopped them to ask for alms, which was a reasonable request, since alms is a small amount of money. Peter looked him squarely in the eyes and instructed the man to pay close attention. The beggar, expecting to receive what he had requested, gave the Apostle his full attention. Peter said, "Silver and gold have I none, but such as I have, give I thee, in the name of Jesus Christ of Nazareth, rise up and walk" (Acts 3:16). Immediately his feet and ankle bones received strength. The scripture says the man went walking and leaping into the temple, praising God. It never occurred to the lame man before to seek God's healing grace, so he asked for small amounts of money since his aspirations were bound by his material limitations. He sat every day at the gateway to a house of prayer. He sat at the very threshold of the power of God and never allowed the Holy Spirit to truly lift him up.

That same power is still capable of lifting African Americans above adversity. When Maya Angelou points out that even in the face of great resistance "Still I Rise," she is celebrating the historical presence of the Holy Spirit in the lives of African people. It is because of the spirit of God within us that we continue to rise. With all else we do, we must begin to nourish our spirit, to open our hearts and minds and find ways to include God in our endeavors. We can begin by always being conscious of our divine nature. When speaking to the Corinthians, Paul spoke of humankind's divinity. He said, "Know ye not that ye are the Temple of God and that the spirit of God dwelleth in you" (1 Co.3:16)? The Temple of God is holy. "Which Temple are you?"

When we clearly understand that God always dwells within us, then we can enjoy abundant life more consistently. Our divinity requires us to avoid self-destructive behavior at all times. There is no place nor time in our lives for jealousy, envy, or abuse of any kind—not drug abuse, wife abuse, or child abuse. There is no time for drunkenness or hedonism. Instead, we must make nourishing the spirit with prayer and meditation a priority.

The Apostle Paul has already advised us to surround ourselves with beauty, to read and study those things of good report. I want to be clear, the power to overcome evil comes from God. It is not some vague higher power. It is not a universal force. It is not a higher consciousness. His name is Jesus!

We are in need of extraordinary power, *therefore*, we should humble ourselves and seek God's face. All that we desire is possible. As stated at the very outset of this book, there is much that is still of great value in the African American community. There is much that is of great value in the hearts of African American people throughout the Diaspora. We have examined ideas and strategies that can cause that value to increase and produce a great people, allowing us to reclaim our place alongside the other great peoples of the world. There is much that African people are equipped to accomplish.

Therefore

But as the Jackson Southerniers sing, "Ain't no power like Holy Ghost power. You need to try it sometime."

NOTES

NOTES

NOTES

NOTES

NOTES